The Devil & Dr. Church

The Devil
& Dr. Church

A Guide to Hell for
Atheists and True Believers

by F. Forrester Church

1817

Harper & Row, Publishers, San Francisco

Cambridge, Hagerstown, New York, Philadelphia
London, Mexico City, São Paulo, Singapore, Sydney

FIRST EDITION

Library of Congress Cataloging-in-Publication Data

Church, F. Forrester.
  The Devil & Dr. Church.

  1. Devil.   2. Hell.   3.Good and evil.   I. Title.
II. Title: Devil and Doctor Church.
BT981.C49 1986   235'.47   85-45714
ISBN 0-06-061371-8

86 87 88 89 90 HC 10 9 8 7 6 5 4 3 2 1

To Peter, Holly, Bob, and Hays
my friends

Contents

Author's Preface

There are many possible reasons to write a book about the devil, but the only good reason to read one is if the author knows what he's about. Three hundred years ago Jakob Boehme, the German mystic, offered the devil's own explanation for his fall from grace and God's subsequent enmity toward him. "I wanted to be an author," Satan explained.*

Apart from wanting to be an author, my other credentials for writing this book are mixed. Among them can be numbered at least four of the seven deadly sins (I am weak on anger, envy, and avarice). I am a husband, deeply in love with his wife, whose eye wanders from time to time, and a father who adores yet often neglects his children. I am a citizen of a free country who is quicker to exercise his freedom than act upon his responsibility; an inveterate moralist who rationalizes his own behavior; and, extending the temptation to confess, a confessor who recognizes that, given how quickly others leap to admire those brazen enough to flaunt their sins, confession is not always an honest act.

On the other hand, my better nature also has its play.

This said, I am not as tormented as perhaps I ought to be, which is the only reservation I have about writing this book. If I knew the devil half as well as the devil knows me, my blood pressure would not be that of a teenager.

---

*Sources for quotations are listed at the end of this book.

The idea for this book belongs to Clayton E. Carlson, Vice President and Publisher of Harper & Row, San Francisco,who thought that "a civilized little book on the devil" might prove provocative. I hope that what follows is not *too* civilized. After all, as Shakespeare reminds us, "The prince of darkness is a gentleman." Actually, this should give us courage—those of us especially whose manners, thoughts, or behavior tend to stray from the acceptable norm.

Let me offer fair warning: what follows is a romp through hell. As G. K. Chesterton reminds us, "Angels can fly because they can take themselves lightly." By the same token, one reason demons fall is because of their gravity. Fortunately, as the old adage has it, "God cannot be mocked." But the devil can, and so can we. It just stands to reason, what is not good for the devil is good for us.

My thesis is a simple one. The devil exists, by nature is a deceiver, and, accordingly, is manifest where we least expect to find him. In turn, the devil's greatest accomplishment is to lead us to believe that he does not exist; his most successful ruse is to cloak himself in virtue; and his favorite guises commend him in ways that impress us, such as patriotism, nationalism, freedom, tolerance, respectability, sophistication, and piety. The devil's true nature is evil disguised as good—which is simply to say, he almost always appears in drag.

This is not a history of the devil. It is not a book of pop psychology, new theology, or transcendental sociology. It is nothing more than one man's struggle with the power of evil in his own heart and the world around him. Because I am a person, for me the devil is a personal agent. I may know little about who I am, why I am here, where I have come from, or where I am going, but evil is a part of all that I do know, even as good is. If I did not believe in the devil, I could not believe in God.

This is not to say that the devil is equal to God. By ancient reckoning, which I accept, the devil is a part of God, that part which has fallen. In the same way, evil is not equal to good. It is a perversion of good, even perhaps an extension of goodness beyond its own perfect limits. There is no good that is not capable of being wrenched from its own context, elevated and perverted into evil. That is what idolatry is all about, a part of the whole that is elevated into something disproportionate and therefore destructive. Graven images, the ancients called them. Today they go by such names as justice, liberty, and honor.

By the same token, even as God contains the devil, the devil is a part of God. And that is our only hope. The odds are long, but if the devil is not curbed and tamed we shall all be damned by the offspring of our genius: self-deception, self-destruction, and, pride. There was a time when only God could have sponsored either genesis or the apocalypse. Today we ourselves possess the powers of creation through genetic engineering, and the powers of Armageddon through the splitting of the atom. To paraphrase John Kennedy's Inaugural Address, here on earth God's work has truly become our own. That goes for the devil in spades.

One more thing. This book, though expressly written for both athiests and true believers, is designed to please neither group. Orthodox and fundamentalist alike will find it blasphemous, and my liberal friends will find it treasonous, ridden with superstition. I am perfectly willing to admit the truth in both claims. After all, blasphemy and treason offer the perfect frame for any honest book about the devil.

I shall begin with an introductory chapter, which you could very well skip if you are more interested in the devil than in my particular problems with him. The heart of the book will be devoted to defining the devil's nature and practice as best I can, after which I shall offer a "Natural Diabology" fashioned to correspond with the principles of natural theology, while taking into account the evil that is incarnate in creation.

Throughout, my point of view is instructed by paradox. To find God or the devil we should always first look where we least expect to find them.

I dedicate this little book to my four closest friends: Peter Fenn, Holland Hendrix, Robert G. Cox, and Hays Rockwell. One is a political consultant, one a professor of religion, one a corporate executive, and one an Episcopal priest. All of them are dangerously successful.

Usually an author takes this opportunity to absolve from any blame those whom he or she has listed in the credits, but in this case my friends each should be reminded that they are partly responsible for everything here that offends them.

1. The Care and Feeding of the Devil

Evil is terribly real for each individual. If you regard the principle of evil as a reality, you can just as well call it the devil.

CARL JUNG

I must confess, I believe in the devil. I've experienced his subtle infiltration of my innermost being and done battle with him in long, dark nights of the soul too often not to believe. That my devil doesn't have horns takes nothing away from the damage he inflicts upon me. With the subtlest of stratagems he leads me into temptation. Under the most transparent of pretexts he still somehow manages to deliver me unto evil.

One day he will be witty, winsome, and alluring. And I, being human, am all too ready to chase the wild geese of his devising. The next day he will be mournful, conspiratorial, and plaintive. And I will follow him down to the abyss, poisoned with the tincture of bitterness, or pitying myself to the point of full submission.

He schemes with me whenever I search for a rationalization to justify doing what I know is wrong. He worms his way into my happiness, beseeching me to throw off contentment and beg for something more. He befriends me in my moments of disenchantment, flattering me with the bittersweet notion that I am a victim who cannot escape from the traps that life has laid for me.

The devil has his attractive side, of course. For one thing, he is relatively easy to please. Although his appetites are insatiable, his tastes are varied. That is to say, he is not picky. Deny him one thing and he will simply ask for something else. For instance, if I deny the devil nicotine, he begs for alcohol. Refused a drink, he wants to smoke but will settle for seven cups of coffee. The devil enjoys the anxiety brought on by too much caffeine.

The one thing that the devil hates, however, is when I devote myself to some object more engrossing than that of my own immediate gratification. When this happens, try as he will, he cannot get my attention. And then he languishes.

Another thing about the devil: he likes to be beaten— that is, flagellated, not overcome. It gives him a sense of self-importance. In fact, the more you beat the devil the stronger he gets. Franz Kafka somewhere said that one of the Devil's most effective tricks to waylay us is to pick a fight with us. It is like a fight with a woman which ends in bed. This is one of the reasons the devil is so fond of religious fanatics.

In addition to religious fanatics, the devil does appear to have a number of clear preferences when it comes to personality types. On the one hand he has a heyday with the pleasure seekers, especially those who would drown out the echoing emptiness within them by turning up the volume of the material world that surrounds them, racing from distraction to distraction, frenetically changing tunes but with each a decibel louder than the last.

There is another kind of pleasure seeker as well, though one might not guess it by observation. These people insist upon doing only what they want, never doing anything but that which they know will please them. The devil laps this up because he knows that over time less and less will please them. Gradually they will withdraw into their tiny little shells, given over to the only pleasure left to them: judging others to be knaves or fools.

Ironically, the devil's fortunes also rest with the pleasure deniers. These people know that life is hell because they remind themselves so often. They know that life is terrifying because they are afraid. They know that life is filled with conspiracy and peopled with conspirators because they are suspicious of everything and everyone. They are victims. They wallow in self-pity. Their little hearts are bitten with envy and bitterness. In the end, only the devil loves them, and it is only the devil whom they love.

Walt Kelly's Pogo sums it up like this. "There is no need to sally forth, for it remains true that those things which make us human are, curiously enough, always close at hand. Resolve then, that on this very ground, with small flags waving and tinny blasts on tiny trumpets, we shall meet the enemy, and not only may he be ours, he may be us."

Let me offer a bit of personal testimony. I recall one particular day when it seemed that everything was coming down on me. Mostly little things: a vicious letter from someone I had never met; yet another in a series of irate phone calls questioning my pivotal role in a conspiracy I could not help but doubt the very existence of; word that someone was angry with me for something that someone else had done; and all topped off by a summons to appear as the defendant in a preliminary hearing to determine whether I had discriminated against Filipino Catholics by firing a woman who, in two weeks as my secretary, had gotten away with everything but her typewriter. In short, it was one of those days. And I was feeling, well ... I was feeling perse-cuted, the innocent and much-aggrieved party in all suits pending then and there in my life, the victim of ignorance, malevolence, and red tape all rolled into one.

So what did I do? I fumed. I pondered all manner of petty, if appropriate, retribution. I complained to everyone who was polite enough to hear me out. Then I had a couple of drinks, which did not help. I took out my frustrations on my wife, Amy. I tried to read but could not concentrate. And then I went to bed but could not sleep. Finally, after tossing and turning and stewing over each of these things in turn, tormenting myself with the furies of my own pas-sion, I fell asleep.

What dreams I had. Courtroom scenes of high and chilling drama; all of my enemies in attendance waving telephone receivers and cheering on the merciless prose-cution witnesses; and other things too terrible, or simply too unsuitable to mention. An absolutely awful night. When morning came, I had no interest whatsoever in facing the day. I'm sure you know the feeling. When this happens to me (as it does on occasion, but rarely with such provoca-tion), Amy has a no-nonsense method of making the bed until there is no room left in it. So, since I was already up, grudgingly I went off to my office.

I don't know why, but by the time I arrived at my office a strange calm had settled over me. My mind was clear of the demons that so recently had been dancing through it. I sat in peace, and for a time thought of nothing but how wonderfully refreshing it felt. Then, never one to be fully content with a good thing, I began to test my new state of mind by inspecting, one by one, the problems of the day before.

Interestingly—this should come as no great surprise—they appeared in an entirely different light. Each was much less serious than it had seemed. One or two even had a kind of dark humor about them, dark yes, but humor nonetheless. A little laughter goes a long way in liberating us from our bunkers.

If an enemy is one who holds it in his or her power to do us harm, as it turned out those whom I felt had wronged me turned out not to be my real enemies. The real enemy was within myself. Their actions may have supplied me with the poison, but from that point on I was free to administer it, refill the prescription, and make myself not only permanently miserable but also magnificently ineffectual.

Shakespeare knew this so very well. Think of his great tragic heroes. Othello is the victim of his own jealousy; Lear, of irrationality and misdirected suspicions; and, Hamlet succumbs on account of his indecisiveness. Each had his enemies, but none compared in sheer destructive power to the enemy lurking within the hero himself.

This is not to say that in Shakespeare's eyes there is no way out. Take this passage from *The Tempest*. Prospero, in reflecting upon his feeling toward his enemies, says: "Though with their high wrongs I am struck to the quick, yet with my nobler reason gainst my fury do I take part."

As Elizabethan scholar E. M. W. Tillyard points out, among the Elizabethans such "is the great condition of success in the spiritual warfare. For the chief enemy is within ourselves and if we do not understand him we cannot be victorious."

The name we give to the enemy within doesn't really matter. "Devil" is as good as any and better than most. At least it offers a graphic and unequivocal image of what we're dealing with. "Know thyself," the Greeks remind us. Very well. In ignorance of ourselves—due so often, I may add, to our preoccupation with the faults of others—not only do we fail to tap our abundant potential for good, but we also remain blind to our enormous capacity for evil.

Let's consider another illustration.

Have you ever put a hex on anybody? I mean an honest-to-goodness hex, double-whammy, pins in dolls, and all of that? Black magic works, you know. The hex is put on, secret words chanted over a brew of herbs, or three hot pins plunged in the heart of a doll, and—if he believes—the victim wastes away, shrivels up, and dies.

But if others can convince him that the hex has been reversed through some countervailing magic of their own, if they can convince him that the spell has been broken, he will recover at once. His appetite will return to him, and then his strength and lust for life. He will thrive again. And, what is more, having so triumphed, he will never be susceptible to the same deadly hex a second time.

You can argue that black magic is all in the mind. Surely you are right. But the things that are in our minds have power, and that power is real, real enough to kill both body and soul.

There is an antidote, and at the end of this little book I shall come back to it. While we have no control over so many of those things ranging from petty to tragic that can befall us, we do have much to say concerning the nature of our response to them. And for this there is only one antidote to counter the infections of self-pity, disaffection, bitterness, suspicion, fear, and despair. It is love. With love, the mind itself can make a heaven of hell, and heaven is the one place where the devil is not allowed.

Unfortunately, we often choose the wrong kind of love. Selfish love leads to self-destruction because its object is too small. And it gets smaller as time goes by, less and less attractive to others, more squalid and pitiful with each passing day. On the other hand the love that leads to self-acceptance, forgiveness of others, and reconciliation with God has an altogether different object, one that grows and grows, its circle expanding until it encompasses all that is animated by the spirit of peace.

It is a love that reminds us that life is precious and to be revered, our life and the lives of those with whom we share the fragility and mystery of being. It is a love that demands much, recalling us to our obligations to one another, lifting us beyond the level of animal egotism to range in search of higher things. It is a difficult love, but a love that graces the lives of all who know it with a meaning sufficient to answer death without fear and life with works of kindness and deeds of praise.

Which love we choose is up to us. The devil has nothing to do with it. That's what freedom is about. If we lack the determination to make our hell a heaven, there is no god that can save us. But with love in our hearts, love self-accepting and all-forgiving, there is no devil nor demonic legion that can make our heaven a hell.

A kind of magic is at work here as well: we pull the pins out of our own doll; we turn the cup of poison from our lips.

"Fine rhetoric," the devil reminds me. And it is true, I am jumping ahead of my story.

2. Welcome to Hell

The safest road to Hell is the gradual one—the gentle slope, soft underfoot, without sudden turnings, without milestones, without signposts.

C. S. LEWIS

Recently, upon suggesting that my six-year-old son mind his manners, I was confronted by this challenge. "Daddy, you don't always mind your manners."

"That's true, Twig."

"And Mommy and Nina don't always mind theirs."

"You're right, they don't."

"Daddy," he proclaimed triumphantly, "even God doesn't have good manners." I must admit, this left me at a complete loss.

"What do you mean God doesn't have good manners?" I asked.

"Daddy," Twig explained to me somewhat impatiently, "if God is inside of us, then God *makes us* not say 'please' and 'thank you.'"

How do you figure it? After six years of exposure to the free spirit of Unitarianism, my son turns out to be a Calvinist! In my attempt to counter this heresy, I quickly discovered what I should already have known. It is impossible to have a meaningful discussion concerning the freedom of the will with a six-year-old.

As I thought about it further, once again I realized that I had learned something unexpected from an off-the-wall conversation with one of my children. For, if Jesus is right,

God doesn't have good manners. He rewards the last laborer to arrive in the vineyard equally with him who had worked the day long. He insults the prudent, pious son by receiving back the prodigal with open arms. He gives precedence in the realm of heaven to prostitutes and tax collectors. No, the one with good manners is not God. It is the devil whose manners are impeccable.

Let me offer an illustration.

The greatest travelogue of a soul in English literature is John Bunyan's *Pilgrim's Progress*. Bunyan's pilgrim is named Christian. His quest is for salvation, to flee from worldly snares and fleshly distractions and secure eternal bliss in the great hereafter.

In Bunyan's allegory, Christian makes it to heaven, but not without many harrowing adventures along the way. He struggles through the famous (if unpronounceable) Slough of Despond; ascends with great trouble the Hill of Difficulty; traverses the Valley of Humility; battles with pagan, pope, and demon; plucks up his courage in crossing the Valley of the Shadow of Death; and survives, most notably and memorably, the many allures of that great city Vanity, with its unsurpassed fair. Really, if you don't mind happy or predictable endings, it's not a bad story. My illustration, however, is based a on a little-known but fascinating tale inspired directly by it: Nathaniel Hawthorne's "The Celestial Rail-road."

You see, in the intervening centuries an extraordinary thing has happened. The enterprising citizens of the City of Destruction have constructed a railroad between this populous and flourishing town and the Celestial City.

Think of the advantages. First, one doesn't have to shoulder one's burden; it can be placed in the baggage compartment. And listen to what they did about the Slough of Despond. They built a bridge over it. Mr. Smooth-it-away, Hawthorne's guide, describes how they turned this Slough of Despond, a disgrace to all the neighborhood, into a foundation sufficient for the bridge's pylons: "by throwing into the slough some editions of books of morality, volumes of French philosophy and German rationalism, tracts, sermons, and essays of modern clergymen, extracts from Plato, Confucius, and various Hindu sages, together with a few ingenious commentaries upon texts of Scripture—all of which, by some scientific process, have been converted into a mass like granite."

This is just one of the wonderful things that has been done to streamline the modern pilgrim's trek to the Celestial City. For instance, they cut a tunnel through the Hill of Difficulty and used the excavated dirt as landfill for the Valley of Humiliation. Later in the journey another troublesome valley, the Valley of the Shadow of Death, was blocked from view by a quadruple row of lamps lining each side of the tracks. These lamps cast a somewhat eerie glow, but at least we are now diverted from having to contemplate the stark reminders of mortality that litter the valley below.

Most marked of all, at least in Hawthorne's view, was the comportment of the pilgrims themselves.

By the aspect and demeanor of these persons it was easy to judge that the feeling of the community had undergone a very favorable change in reference to the Celestial pilgrimage. It would have done Bunyan's heart good to see it. Instead of a lonely and ragged man with a huge burthen on his back, plodding along sorrowfully on foot while the whole city hooted after him, here were parties of the first gentry and most respectable people in the neighborhood setting forth towards the Celestial City as cheerfully as if the pilgrimage were merely a summer tour. Among the gentlemen were characters of deserved eminence, magistrates, politicians, and men of wealth, by whose example religion could not but be greatly recommended to their meaner brethren. . . . There was much pleasant conversation about the news of the day, topics of business, politics, or the lighter matters of amusement; while religion, though indubitably the main thing at heart, was thrown tastefully into the back-ground.

There was only one problem with this wonderful railroad. While it simplified the religious journey in oh-so-many ways—offering shortcuts, sparing one both from the giddy heights and the harrowing depths of experience and consciousness as well as from all troublesome pangs of conscience—one problem remained. Its final stop was not heaven, as promised. It was hell.

If the devil trades almost flawlessly in anything, it is deceit. His finest trick is to dress us up in our Sunday best and point us toward the abyss. How well I can imagine myself in the club car on this train bound for hell. In fact, you and I might find ourselves there together, first exchanging pleasantries, then commiserating over the news of the day.

It's just the sort of thing the devil loves, especially our tendency toward smug and self-righteous moral posturing. Not that we waste too much time on it—hors d'oeuvres are being served. They deserve at least as much attention as the opposition party's latest planet-threatening gaff.

So begins our journey, with this brief introduction to the "hell as a successful cocktail party" school of criticism, one of several to which I subscribe. Surround yourself with attractive acquaintances, tackle some important topic, express your opinion passionately (insofar as it neither inconveniences you nor makes others uncomfortable), and welcome to hell.

Like myself, Nathaniel Hawthorne was a Unitarian, though his roots were tangled deep in the loam of the unconscious, which most of his Unitarian contemporaries found too dank and mealy for their cultivation. In fact, he wrote "The Celestial Rail-road" as a satire upon the high Unitarian fashions of his day.

Hawthorne was more a critic than a practitioner of Unitarianism. But he was divided in his loyalties. On the one hand he knew that evil is so subtly woven into the human fabric that even his most committed liberal friends, in their zeal to reform, simply had not the eye to perceive it. And apart from the reformers, who invested their new-found freedom by acting responsibly, most Unitarians—like most Episcopalians and Presbyterians and every other stripe of mainline Protestant today—were far too busy enjoying their liberation from the eternal punishment for sin to contemplate either the burden innate sinfulness placed upon them or the terror of their lives' emptiness.

On the other hand, the old theology was as blasphemous in its pieties as the new was sacrilegious in its lack of them. So, rather than choose between the two, Hawthorne simply told stories. In one, "The Minister's Black Veil," Hawthorne's protagonist, having become aware of the monstrosity of his own sinful nature, puts a black veil on his face and wears it to the end of his days. It is a universal symbol. "I look around me," he says, "and, lo! on every visage a Black Veil!"

This almost brings us up to date. Just following World War II, after 6 million Jews had been herded into boxcars, stripped, shot or gassed, and incinerated in ovens all across Eastern Europe, Thomas Mann wrote his own *Dr. Faustus*. "The scientific superiority of liberal theology, it is now said, is indeed incontestable," Mann's narrator notes, "but its theological position is weak, for its moralism and human-ism lack insight into the daemonic character of human existence."

The same can be said for much of that which passes for religion—often private or non-institutional—here in the United States today. Speaking especially of the new reli-gions, but touching upon a truth that is far more wide-spread, Henry Fairlie, in his book *The Seven Deadly Sins Today,* writes:

> It is characteristic of our age that people want to have God but do not want to have the Devil. People are inventing gods for themselves, with what I have elsewhere called their Do-It-Yourself God Kits. But they are gods who do not demand much of them, and they certainly are not gods who punish, although they are allowed to reward. On the contrary, their gods absolve them from conflict and doubt, massage them, pat them on the head, and . . . tell them to run along, get stoned if they will, pick marigolds, and love. So easy it is to love! But above all they are gods who will not trouble them with the fact of evil. The problems of evil, suffering, and death are not confronted, but evaded and dismissed.

In the struggle for our nation's soul, liberal religion was not vanquished, it triumphed. There was a time in the mid-nineteenth century when Universalism, whose creed was that hell did not exist and all would be saved, was the fastest-growing religion in America. And then something happened. It stopped growing. It and Unitarianism—whose creed was similar, namely, that human beings are by nature good and fall only on account of improper nurture, culture, and education—both plummeted into a precipitous decline that has lasted until this very day.

This was not because the popular belief in hell saw a

resurgence, though revivals continue. It was not even because the sanitized view of human nature sponsored by liberal religion failed to hold the public imagination. It did hold. What happened was that the liberals won.

Think about it.

All the mainline, establishment, nonfundamentalist religions quietly dropped hell and the devil from their menus. Each was still available for dread contemplation by special order, and if you asked the chef he might even recommend them to you; but in actual practice hell and the devil all but disappeared. A century's worth of sermons and devotional tracts tells the tale.

Of course, the real victory was won elsewhere. The secular philosophy, which though embattled dominates to this day, turns out to be very much in line with the original teachings of liberal reformers, who cared far more about the triumph of their philosophy than they did about the triumph of their faith. In the meantime, as Prime Minister Gladstone of Great Britain summed it up at the end of the nineteenth century, the doctrine of hell had been "relegated to the far off corners of the Christian mind . . . there to sleep in deep shadow as a thing needless in our enlightened and progressive age."

I must admit the above paragraphs could be quoted by fundamentalists who are ever seeking proof for what they term "the secular humanist conspiracy that threatens to destroy our country." Instead, I would invite them to consider themselves, for just as every book on the devil should begin at home, a stone well-aimed at the devil is best thrown at a mirror.

In fact, the devil has long since grown bored with liberal religion. Today, we serve his purpose primarily by not recognizing his existence, even as his purpose was served by Hitler's unwitting, self-deceiving collaborators—not only in Germany and abroad, but in Washington, in the White House—who closed their eyes, their hearts, and their gates while the Jews burned in Europe.

This, of course, is passive evil. Active evil is more distinctive, but also more blatant; it is important, but not the only important part of the devil's story. A few decades ago it was written by Stalin in his gulag and the Führer in his ovens. Today it is being written by all those true-believers who, with bigotry and zeal, employ the powers of the present age—religion, the state, ideology, television, bombs—as they too embark, one tribe after another, upon their holy crusades to cleanse the world.

"Fight for the religion of God," the Koran reads, and so diehard believers do: hijacking planes, blowing up cars, driving trucks filled with dynamite into buildings filled with people. Instant heaven, smiling all the way.

"I have not come to bring peace, but a sword," Jesus is quoted (Matt. 10:34), and certain loyal followers respond: bombing abortion clinics; lobbying for capital punishment; helping the president with his interpretation of the book of Revelation, so that "sufficient" armaments will be stockpiled for our final battle with the "Evil Empire."

Since almost all such people proclaim themselves to be fighting for God and against Satan, it is often hard to sort the players out, especially if we only observe their actions. In *The Devil's Dictionary,* Ambrose Bierce defines "infidel" as follows: "in New York, one who does not believe in the Christian religion; in Constantinople, one who does." We all are skilled in disassociating ourselves from guilt, blame, or sin—take your pick—by assigning it to those whom we are predisposed to view in negative terms.

Writing in *Newsweek* magazine about the People's Temple cult one week after the mass "Kool-Aid" suicide of Jim Jones and his "children" in Guyana, syndicated columnist Meg Greenfield pointed out how people she knew were managing to rationalize the horror in such a way that it would make sense to them. Some, themselves not religious, said that it was the fault of religious belief; conservatives claimed that it was the fault of left-wing radicalism; and radicals responded that the victims had been driven to despair by the right-wing racism of capitalist society.

Such pat explanations, Greenfield writes, make "the night less frightening" and serve to "tame and domesticate the horror by making it fit our prejudices and predilections." But she concludes that in fact the horror arose from "the dark impulses that lurk in every private psyche. . . . The jungle is only a few yards away."

This is a discomfiting thought for rationalists, especially for religious liberals, to consider—even harder to do anything constructive about. That, of course, is precisely it. The devil's half-nelson. As we survey the evils of the world we are not prompted, as our forebears were, to go out and do something. We feel overwhelmed. Really, what could we do? Instead, ours is the respectable sin of sophisticated resignation. Before, when we knew what was right, we went straight out and did something about it. Today we are more likely to know what is wrong and leap, out of habit, to the reluctant if convenient conclusion that, indeed, we *can't* do anything about it—save, perhaps, preaching a strongly worded sermon or displaying our wit while deriding our political opponents in casual conversation so that everyone will know which side we're on.

Even progress, the true faith of most nineteenth-century liberals, has come a cropper. B. F. Skinner, one of the most eloquent latter-day apostles of human rationality as the ultimate panacea for all of society's ills, has said of our flirtation with nuclear annihilation, "The argument that we have always solved our problems in the past and shall therefore solve this one is like reassuring a dying man by pointing out that he has always recovered from his illnesses."

So here we are, on our way straight to hell. As the devil trumps out his best religious finery for bigots and goons, stealing God's march under God's own banner, for us liberals he dons designer sackcloth and ashes and pours out a Perrier and lime. Just another evening, just another cocktail party in the first-class quarters on the train to oblivion.

3. The Cunning Livery of Hell

Had he been obliged always to act the mere devil in his own clothes, and with his own shape, appearing uppermost in all cases and places, he could never have preached in so many pulpits, presided in so many councils, voted in so many committees, sat in so many courts, and influenced so many parties and factions in church and state.

DANIEL DEFOE

I suppose that many of us have trouble believing in the devil for the same reason that we have trouble believing in God. The God we disbelieve in is an anthropomorphic, paternalistic greatbeard in the clouds. The devil we disbelieve in is a trim, middle-aged gent with horns, goatee, and a forked tail, who has a penchant for red, tight-fitting clothing.

It is as easy to torch a straw devil as it is to torch a straw god. In both instances the devil will congratulate us for our admirable lack of superstition and strike the match. As Baudelaire reminds us, "The Devil's most beautiful ruse is to convince us that he does not exist." What better way to accomplish this than by dancing about in the popular imagination as a trick-or-treater?

Really, can you even begin to take seriously any scoundrel who passes himself off under such nicknames as Hopdance, Rosenkranz, Black Jack, Beelzebub, Brendly, Bellie Blind, Old Scratch, Old Bogie, Old Boots, Old Harry, Old Chap, and Old Nick? Good fellow, the devil, hale and well met.

That the devil as popularly depicted does not exist, of course, is almost completely beside the point. To recognize the devil requires a little imagination, but nothing fanciful. Put that debonair fellow with a twinkle in his eye and a pitchfork in his hand out of your mind. Like God, the devil is precisely where one least expects to find her.

Just try to sniff her out or convict her by her clothes. I warn you, she is not heavily perfumed. More likely she smells sweet as a baby fresh from the bath. And what finery she wears. Simple yet elegant; in a word, understated. Nothing outlandish. Her hems are the right length and she only wears a hat when a hat is appropriate. As for him, his suits are well-pressed, his shoes have a comfortable day-old shine, and he doesn't flash his money.

If the devil is particularly enamored of his Halloween image, there is another ruse that he finds even more useful, and that is to distract us by donning the cloak of evil itself. Think about it. Could you imagine a better trick to lure your victims away from the evil in their own lives and its relationship to the evil in the world around them than to paint an obvious monster in the corner where everyone can see it? Dress it up as a mugger, a punk rocker, a communist; or take a sexually loaded disease like AIDS or herpes. Anything to distract us from our own daily complicity in sin.

The popular conception of the devil as depicted in most Western art and literature is a medieval amalgam. In Jakob Grimm's description, "He is at once of Jewish, Christian, heathen, elfish, gigantic and spectral stock." The generic form the devil takes is that of a black, hairy, disfigured, flying creature; half-man, half-bat or half-dragon; with horns, a forked tail, long pointed ears, and claws on his hands and feet. In almost every instance his beastly nature is overt. Not unlike the Gorgon of Greek mythology, renderings of Satan (to paraphrase Anatole France) represent the sympathetic alliance between physical ugliness and moral evil. Dante enthrones a grotesque three-faced giant in his hell. You couldn't miss him if you tried. In Western folklore, black is the color of evil. The devil appeared to St. Anthony in the desert once in the form of a black giant, his head touching the clouds, and once in the form of a naked black child. In his sixteenth century tome, *The Discoverie of Witchcraft,* Reginald Scot claims that of all human forms, demons most favor that of a Negro or a Moor. By the same token, the term "printer's devil" was coined near the end of the fifteenth century, when the great Venetian printer Aldus Manutius employed in his shop a black slave whom townsfolk fingered as an imp from hell.

We are not unfamiliar with this tendency in our own literature. For instance, the devil pops up as a black bogey in Washington Irving's story "The Devil and Tom Walker." That, of course, was a century and a half ago. Years later, approaching the advent of our own enlightened age, Arturo Graf, in *The Story of the Devil*, explains why. "Black appears as the native color of the demons from the very earliest centuries of Christianity, and the reasons for assigning it to them are self-explanatory, so obvious are they, and natural."

He would have been shocked, I am sure, to discover that in many countries in West Africa the devil prefers to be white. Or to encounter the Oriental curse "as white as the devil." In the Orient white is the color of death and mourning. All of which makes for a rather interesting object lesson. What better role for the devil to play than to assist us in feeding our prejudices? Perhaps, as the old saying goes, "the devil is not so black as he is painted."

Much of what we think we know about the devil comes from medieval saints. We have a wide selection to choose from, but a single example should suffice. Saint Guthlac, an English hermit, described the devils of his acquaintance as having huge heads, long necks, thin, swarthy countenances, squalid beards, bushy ears, lowering brows, savage eyes, teeth like horses', singed locks, wide mouths, bulging breasts, scraggly arms, knock-knees, bow legs, unwieldy heels, and splayed feet. And, if this were not enough to strike the fear of God in any mortal, they also had loud, hoarse voices, and from their mouths they vomited flames.

Recognizing the devil would not be all that difficult if he were to make a habit of appearing in such diabolical guise. That, by the way, is precisely what is wrong with the popular demonology. By nature the devil is a liar, camouflaged in the fashion of the times, impossible to pick out in a crowd. There is much destruction in this world,—fires, earthquakes, floods—that the devil has nothing to do with. The devil's trademark is not evil dressed as evil, but evil dressed as good.

If more widespread, such insights as this could lead to a considerable amount of long-overdue revisionist demonography. For instance, the story is told by many medieval writers of a painter who portrayed the devil in such an unflattering manner—twisted, dark, gnarled, ugly, altogether gruesome—that the devil himself hurled the painter down from the scaffolding just when the poor fellow was putting the finishing touches on his splendid work. Fortunately, a madonna, whom the painter had portrayed as very beautiful, leapt from the fresco and caught the painter in her outstretched arms, thus sparing him from certain death.

I suspect that tradition has the players' roles reversed

here. Why would the devil, who is not at all ugly, and in fact seeks to appear beautiful, not wish to have himself portrayed in such a way as to further ensure that no suspicion whatsoever would be cast upon him? To be known as he is would crimp his style, which is to ravish the world as inconspicuously as possible.

Let me retell the story as I expect it really happened. The truth is that the clumsy painter slipped and was about to fall to a premature death, thus robbing the devil of one more unwitting agent here on earth. So the devil did what he does best. He disguised himself—in this instance as the Virgin Mary—leapt from the ceiling, and saved his servant just before the unfortunate young man hit the floor. Even as the devil himself might have predicted, the painter then went out and told his friends of this wondrous miracle. In a single stroke the devil had thus multiplied his gain. The story was repeated hundreds of times, and the devil's anonymity further assured.

It just goes to show (present company included), you shouldn't believe everything you read.

Admittedly, not every medieval commentator was in the devil's hire. A few saw the devil for what he is: deceptively attractive. In the fifteenth century Bishop Federigo Frezzi of Foligno, author of the *Quadriregio,* wrote of his surprise when, upon encountering Satan in hell, he discovered instead of a monster a creature of great beauty.

> I thought to see a monster foul, uncouth;
> I thought to see a realm all waste and sad:
> And him I saw triumphant, glorious.
> Stately he was, and fair, and so benign
> His aspect, and with majesty so filled,
> That of all reverence he appeared most worthy.

Here we meet Lucifer, the rebel angel, beautiful, proud, fallen from grace but not without graces of his own: Lucifer, the light bearer, the morning star, *hillel* in Hebrew, the planet Venus, brightest of luminaries, appearing above the eastern horizon prior to daybreak and surpassing in brilliance all other stars and planets in the firmament. "How art thou fallen from heaven, O Lucifer, son of the morning! How art thou cut down to the ground, which didst weaken the nations," Isaiah cries (Ia. 14:12 KJV).

The notion of a heavenly rebellion is common to most mythologies. In Persian mythology Ahriman, who fought against Ormuzd, was bound for a thousand years. Among the Greeks Prometheus, who stole the fire of the Gods from Zeus and gave it to mortals, is chained to a rock, his liver picked by a vulture night after night forever. Vrita and Indra struggle in Hindu mythology, Set and Horus in the mythology of Egypt. And, in Scandinavian mythology, Loki, the calumniator of the northern gods of Asgardh, is fettered in hell, whence he will return in the "twilight of the gods" to do battle with them and their servants in Valhalla.

The identification of Satan with Lucifer, however, is not explicitly made in the Scriptures. It was fashioned by the early church fathers out of the above passage in Isaiah and another in Ezekiel, which were read according to the ancient tradition. As the story went, the most illustrious of the angels had rebelled against God and fallen from heaven. With this as background, the symbolism in both passages was compelling.

Let's take a brief excursion through the Bible.

Ezekiel mentions a prince of Tyre, a man who became so vain about all of his riches and intelligence that he claimed to be God. If such were the character of the prince, who then was his father, the king?

Ezekiel describes the king of Tyre as follows: "You were the signet of perfection, full of wisdom and perfect in beauty. You were in Eden, the garden of God; every precious stone was your covering. . . . You were on the holy mountain of God; in the midst of the stones of fire you walked. You were blameless in your ways from the day you were created, till iniquity was found in you" (Ezek. 28:11-15).

Among the many possible identifications for Ezekiel's king of Tyre, the one that most often suggested itself to patristic scholars was Lucifer himself. Consider how Lucifer's crime and fate are described by Isaiah: "You said in your heart, 'I will ascend to heaven; above the stars of God I will set my throne on high. . . . But you are brought down to Sheol [hell], to the depths of the Pit"(Isa. 14:13, 15).

Lucifer's sin was the sin of pride. In several medieval mystery plays, he is portrayed as a high official of heaven, seated next to God, but not content even with this lofty perch. God warns him not to touch the divine throne. But he cannot resist. Assuming what he believes to be his own rightful place, he ascends, but only for an instant to enjoy, for at once he is cast from heaven into the abyss by the archangel Michael, ever loyal to God.

Another factor introduced here is the notion that the devil once served as one of God's principal deputies. In Jewish traditions more ancient than those which identify the devil with Lucifer, Satan—translated "diablos" in Greek, "adversary, accuser, calumniator"—is the name of the angel who sits among God's heavenly counselors. He plays, in fact, the role of prosecuting attorney in God's court.

In the trial of the High Priest Joshua, for instance, the defendent stands in the dock "before the angel of the Lord, with Satan standing at his right hand to accuse him" (Zech. 3:1). Satan plays this same role in the book of Job. Still numbered among the angels of heaven, he doubts Job's righteousness and provokes the test that is to plunge God's most faithful servant from the height of happiness into the pit of despair.

One day during a meeting of the court of heaven, God inquires after Satan's recent activites. His prosecuting angel responds that he has been ranging over the earth, evidently seeking out sinners for punishment. "Have you considered my servant Job?" God asks. "There is none like him on the earth, a blameless and upright man, who fears God and turns away from evil." Satan replies that Job has every reason to be faithful. He is prosperous, happily married, and healthy. Take these things away, Satan suggests, and Job "will curse thee to thy face."

Rising to this challenge, God places Job under Satan's power. Before long this faithful man has lost everything he loves. Only his life is spared. Even as God exults in Job's integrity, Job himself is reduced to sitting among the ashes scratching himself with a piece of a broken pot, his flesh festering from head to foot with running sores (Job 1-2).

Though the instigator and agent of Job's distress, Satan here is still acting according to God's will. He is a part of God, the shadow side, to use Carl Jung's suggestive terminology. He is the evil that is part of good. In Job as in Zechariah, Satan personifies not so much evil itself, but rather the destructive side of God's own being.

And then we have the story of the serpent in Genesis. When Satan came to Adam and Eve in the guise of a serpent, the Bible reminds us that "the serpent was more subtle than any other wild creature that the Lord God had made" (Gen. 3:1). He offered something that God did not want Adam and Eve to have, the fruit of the tree of the knowledge of good and evil. His deceit was in claiming that the consequences for this would not be nearly as considerable as God had threatened, namely, the loss of immortality. But, as Eve laments, "The serpent beguiled me, and I ate" (Gen. 3:13).

This story tells us perhaps the most important thing we have to remember about the devil. As the Apostle John writes, "He was a murderer from the beginning, and has nothing to do with the truth, because there is no truth in him. When he lies, he speaks according to his own nature, for he is a liar and the father of lies" (John 8:44). The last judgment upon Satan as recorded in the book of Revelation is rendered accordingly, against "the devil, who had deceived" (Rev. 20:10).

Here, combining the images of Lucifer, Satan, and the serpent, we can finally begin to sketch the devil's nature and personality. He is part of God. He is beautiful. He is proud. He is brilliant. He is destructive, both of self and of others. He is clever. He is wise in the ways of the world. And he is a liar. With this our picture of the Devil "who deceives" begins to emerge from the misleading shadow of his popular image: part monster, "satanic," "diabolical"; and, part petty trickster, the old salamander, rogue, and buffoon.

This is not to say that everyone save an occasional minor poet missed the devil's mark. Perhaps his most telling portrait in all of literature is John Milton's in *Paradise Lost*. Milton's Satan is "majestic though in ruin." He is an object both of admiration and of fear, "the strongest and the fiercest spirit that fought in heaven, now fiercer by despair."

There is no question about it. Satan is Milton's protagonist in *Paradise Lost*. Whether he is also Milton's hero, however, has long been subject to debate. Shelley thought so, as did Byron and Keats. The curse of the romantics was that they lionized anything that reminded them of themselves. And yet, for all his torment, Milton's Satan *is* an impressive character.

> With grave
> Aspect he rose, and in his rising seem'd
> A pillar of state; deep on his front engraven
> Deliberation sat and public care;
> And princely counsel in his face yet shone.

Not to mention the way Milton treats the other demons in hell. Baal, Belial, Dagon, Mammon, Moloch, and Rimmon do not have horns and tails. They are diabolical in the true sense, in a way that we, from our own experience, can identify with and understand.

After Milton, the devil in literature was never quite the same. Here are two examples, both from best-sellers of their day. In the late 1890s Marie Corelli, in her novel *The Sorrows of Satan,* describes the devil as extraordinarily beautiful, fascinating in his manner, robustly healthy, and absolutely brilliant, in short, "the perfect impersonation of perfect manhood." At about the same time, Mark Twain, in his delightfully misanthropic "The Mysterious Stranger," describes Satan—actually the devil's nephew—in equally attractive terms. "He made us forget everything; we could only listen to him and love him and be his slaves, to do with us as he would. He made us drunk with the joy of being with him and of looking into the heaven of his eyes, and of feeling the ecstasy that thrilled along our veins from the touch of his hand."

Both are perhaps overdone, but these two representations of the devil are far more telling than the great majority of those preceding Milton. At least among the literary set, the image of the devil has been given a much needed face-lift.

On the other hand, many of those who protest deep concern about the devil today don't seem to have picked up on this at all. For instance, in recent years there has been a great hue and cry in the right-wing religious press about Satanism. Hal Lindsey, who proclaims himself to be the best-selling author of our time, fulminates in book after book against what he perceives to be a dangerous, if cosmically telling, new rash of witches, warlocks, and wizards practicing their sorcery in our midst. Reading Lindsey and others like him, I am reminded of Daniel Defoe's lament about his own time. "Either the Devil uses us more like fools than he did our ancestors, or we really are worse fools than those ages produced; for they were never deluded by such low-priced devils as we are."

This is not to say that the modern-day witch-hunt is not carried out in deadly earnest. In fact, to advance his own acquaintance with the adversary, Mr. Lindsey even attended a Witchcraft and Sorcery Convention in Los Angeles. "There is a move today," one wizard told him, "to bring witchcraft into the open as a religion." On my own list of things to worry about, the institutionalization of witchcraft is right at the bottom. Even Billy Graham reminds us, "Satan does not want to build a church and call it 'The First Church of Satan.' He is far too clever for that. He invades the Sunday school, the youth department, the Christian education program, the pulpit and the seminary classroom." I might add the corporate board room, the halls of Congress, and the oval office, but one should avoid beginning lists that have no end.

In any event, we can forget witches and wizards. We can forget Hop-dance and Old Nick. We certainly can forget three-faced giants and flying fiends. All we have to remember, as St. Paul himself reminds us, is that "Satan disguises himself as an angel of light. So it is not strange if his servants also disguise themselves as servants of righteousness" (2 Cor. 11:14-15).

4. Idolatries of Good

And out of good still to find means of evil.

JOHN MILTON

In Milton's *Paradise Lost* Satan's rebellion against God begins as a struggle for liberty. Few revolutions do not begin in this manner. Injustice is perceived and liberty sought.

Liberty, liberation, liberalism: they all share the same root, the Latin word that means freedom. Surely freedom is a good thing. With the exception of love, there is none better. Yet, before too long, Satan's own fight for freedom has developed into little more than a petty struggle for "honor, dominion, glory, and renown."

This is the very nature of idolatry. Most idolatry is not devoted to objects that are evil in and of themselves. If this were the case it would not be nearly as seductive and persuasive a phenomenon as it is. But idolatry always begins with something good, things like freedom and art, health and love, sex and patriotism.

It is as easy to fashion a religion out of lofty concepts and principles as it is difficult to practice that religion in such a way that the very good which is being worshiped does not itself become diabolical.

Take tolerance. Now there is a liberal virtue if ever there were one. At its most telling, to tolerate means "to bear with repugnance." The problem is, there are some things so repugnant that we should not bear them. And there are other things, people, or actions that deserve not our tolerance but our active respect. If by tolerance we mean having dinner with our Great Aunt Sally, whom we can't stand, in this limited application it is surely not a bad thing. But what happens when we elevate tolerance into a first principle? Dorothy Sayers tells us: "In the world it calls itself Tolerance, but in hell it is called Despair.... It is the sin which believes in nothing, cares for nothing, seeks to know nothing, interferes with nothing, enjoys nothing, loves nothing, hates nothing, finds purpose in nothing, lives for nothing, and only remains alive because there is nothing it would die for."

Or, take love. How well it is described in these words by William Blake from his poem, "The Clod and the Pebble."

> Love seeketh not itself to please,
> Nor for itself hath any care,
> But for another gives it ease,
> And builds a Heaven in Hell's despair.

And how well Blake describes the perversion, the idolatry, of love in these words from the third stanza of the same poem.

> Love seeketh only self to please,
> To bind another to its delight,
> Joys in another's loss of ease,
> And builds a Hell in Heaven's despite.

Returning to the club car of the *Celestial Express*—whose passengers, with heaven on their itinerary, are destined for hell—here too the idolatries we encounter are as varied as good itself, with each cloaked in its own distinctive garb. Satan wears with equal ease a professor's gown, a three-piece suit, jogging togs, and a clerical robe. That is to say, in addition to being a free-spirited, tolerant lover, the devil is also sophisticated, respectable, self-satisfied, and pious.

Not that any of these things is inherently bad. It's just that the devil finds a way to pervert them. He trades in sophistication, hoping to make us forget our natural kinship with others; in respectability, primarily to encourage us to subdue our independent opinions; in self-satisfaction, helping us fill ourselves without spilling over for others; and in piety, simply for the hell of it. Of all things, religion is by far the easiest to pervert. Like the devil himself, its perversions are "legion."

First let's consider sophistication, the cultivation of special knowledge expressly for cultural purposes. While possession of such knowledge may enlighten others as well as ourselves, it has a general tendency to lift us above others. We begin to think better of ourselves than we do of them, and end up squandering our energy on the finer points of caste distinction.

For instance, there is enormous value in beautiful music, art, and literature. And there is special pleasure to be enjoyed in the appreciation of fine wine or an exquisitely prepared meal. But, as Goethe points out in his *Faust,* "Culture which the whole world licks also the devil sucks." Instead of enjoying these things for their own sake, we twist our pleasure into a tribute to our own discrimination or accomplishment. In short, we become snobs.

Fittingly, the word "sophistication"—from the Greek verb *sophizesthai*—has two very different meanings. Playing on the related but contrasting notions of wisdom and cleverness, it means not only "to be wise," but also "to deceive." On the one hand, in the Scriptures Sophia is the personification of wisdom. On the other, something that is sophisticated is by definition adulterated. For instance, a sophisticated oil is one that no longer exists in its natural, pure, or original state. Since wisdom is an attractive goal and the devil is particularly expert in deceit, sophistication is a natural foil for him. It promises something that will elevate us above others, but delivers us instead straight into the hell of estrangement, jadedness, and disillusion.

If the devil were to have a rallying cry it would be this: "Anything for its own sake." Art for art's sake, for instance. Or knowledge for the sake of knowledge, nothing more.

The potential consequences are spelled out in the legend of Dr. Faustus. In several versions of this tale of a brilliant scholar who sells his soul to the devil in exchange for special knowledge—in this case not cultural, but cosmic— Faust is an alchemist. His ambition is to change lead into gold, but the real alchemy takes place in Faust's own soul.

Respectability, though tending equally toward a deceptively grounded smugness, is altogether different. Here, instead of distinctiveness or superiority, the goal is unadulterated normalcy. Anything considered abnormal is to be scrupulously avoided.

In *The Devil's Dictionary,* Ambrose Bierce defines "abnormal" as follows: "Not conforming to standard. In matters of thought and conduct, to be independent is to be abnormal, to be abnormal is to be detested. Wherefore the lexicographer adviseth a striving toward a straighter resemblance to the Average Man than he hath to himself. Whoso attaineth thereto shall have peace, the prospect of death and the hope of Hell."

To be sure, there are practical advantages to respectability. Having achieved it, we can move easily and inconspicuously in a respectable crowd—almost as if we belonged. The devil loves this, of course. Crowds are his thing.

Think of all the good, respectable, churchgoing Germans and Italians who went along with fascism. Better yet, since the devil is eager for us to look for evil outside our own precincts, think of all the good, respectable, churchgoing Americans who tolerated slavery: not only in the South, where the economy was designed to depend upon it, but in the North as well. In New York City, for instance; in my very church.

For two years in the late 1830s Charles Follen, an outspoken abolitionist, served as the minister of the Unitarian Church of All Souls in New York City. He was an accomplished scholar, a professor of German literature and theology at Harvard. Just the sort of respectable person one might seek when looking for a minister. The problem was, he couldn't hold his tongue. He took the responsibility of a free pulpit very seriously, and when moved to do so spoke out eloquently against any compromise with slavery. This didn't cause a scene. Respectable people don't make a scene. They send a delegation with instructions to thank their minister very much for his services, and then form a committee to find a new minister. And then years later, when explaining to themselves why Charles Follen didn't work out as their minister, they would talk about his German accent. The man was simply impossible to understand.

A third and much-favored cloak for the devil is self-satisfaction. The goal of self-satisfaction is having what we want whenever we want it, without overdoing it, of course (there is nothing satisfying about a hangover). This used to be such an obvious sin—selfishness we called it—that it served the devil very poorly. But not anymore. These days kneeling at the altar of jogging, continuing education, or bean sprouts is much easier than idolizing sex or martinis, especially on the conscience.

Forget the obvious cases. Most of us have been socialized. We know that our satisfaction is in part dependent on others. Not only have we learned to share our toys, but the dominant form of self-satisfaction in our own time even *includes* sharing our toys, as in our homes, our private temples of culture where in twos or threes we gather in our own name to devote our loving attention to trivial pursuits.

The mischief here is subtle but dangerous. It lies in our devotion to doing only what we know will please us, only what we really want to do. In fact, the devil's favorite sermon is to remind us that we deserve whatever we want whenever we want it.

There is only one problem. If we conspire to do only those things that please us, over time less and less will please us. Things that pose any challenge or inconvenience will eventually become too much for us to respond to, even if once they were the wellspring of our creativity. Over the years, as fewer things please us and more things disappoint us, we will find ourselves living in ever-diminishing circles, with only ourselves or people like us for company, and poor, bickering, querulous company at that. As Oscar Wilde once wrote, "In this world there are only two tragedies. One is not getting what one wants, and the other is getting it."

To the extent that we are self-absorbed, we remain relatively useless people. We plant very little outside of our own garden, and even that we fence in and block from others' view. Ultimately, we build our fences so high that even the sunshine is blocked out and our little gardens wither and fade.

The sad thing is not that we will die one day before discovering much real meaning or purpose in our lives. It is that every day we live, our world and our neighbors are diminished by the things we avoid doing. On the other hand, the more you prune a plant, the stronger grow its roots. In the same spirit, wisdom teaches us to empty ourselves and be filled. It's another paradox. We pour ourselves out, filling one another up, and yet our own cup somehow remains brimful and running over. But if we restrain ourselves, trying to save every drop of our own precious nectar, over time it will evaporate and our cup will be dry. We are filled by self-emptying, not by surfeit of self.

Ask yourself this question. When you write a check for a worthy cause, something you believe in, what do you say to yourself? Is it, "Am I giving too little?" or, "Am I giving too much?" For most of us, certainly it is the latter. This is not true of our investments. There we measure one potential value against and commit ourselves as fully as possible to our promised gain.

Not that we don't make a show of whatever we do give, once prudence—another of the devil's favorites—has its say. Widow's mites don't fit on plaques, but there is no lack of wall space for the relatively token generosity of the wealthy. As for the rest of us, the devil will provide a shady place in our hearts for self-satisfaction and piety to meet.

Consider the parable of the Good Samaritan. In Jesus' own day Samaritans were considered anything but good.

In fact they were unclean, the untouchables of their time, certainly not the sort of people that anyone in a responsible position would want to have personal dealings with.

A a man lies wounded by the side of the road. A clergyman walks by without stopping, undoubtedly on his way to an important meeting, the major item on its agenda being next year's annual canvas. Then a politician walks by, also in a hurry, very likely on his way to give a speech on social justice at a political dinner. And then a Samaritan walks by.

To get the full impact of this story think of it not as the parable of the good Samaritan, but rather, depending on your own prejudices, as the parable of the good redneck or the parable of the good homosexual. He stops, cradles the wounded man in his arms, takes him to an inn, cares for him, and gives him money.

Unlike some of Jesus' parables, in this one the moral is obvious. Good is as good does. The pillars of the community—however esteemed, however busily employed sponsoring "good" works, however noble their pretexts for not stopping by the roadside to help a fellow human being in distress—are simply running errands for the devil. On the other hand, the Samaritan, however despised, is good, not by virtue of who he may or may not be, but simply on account of the fact that his actions are good. If Jesus hadn't noticed, his story would never have been told.

Where true piety exists it almost never draws attention to itself. In contrast, I would love to have heard the clergyman praying for God's assistance in the raising of sufficient funds to "do the Lord's work," or the politician pulling the heartstrings of his listeners in rhetorical proof of his compassion for the poor. Then as today, when it came to piety, clergymen and self-righteous politicians served the devil equally well. As Pascal reminds us, "Men never do evil so completely and cheerfully as when they do it from religious convictions."

Someone once said that the worst thing about a bad man is his religion. This can be generalized yet further. For instance, politicians are not inherently bad people, but it could be argued that the worst thing about many of them is their religion. The cloak of piety is particularly insidious when worn by public officials. Not that they necessarily go to church. No matter. To hear certain politicians tell it, they know just what God wants: prayer in the public schools; a ban on abortions; and a massive increase in the defense budget.

Each of these is a serious issue, but when public officials use their pulpits to suggest that God is on their side, it is frightening. Over the centuries more unadulterated evil, carnage, and violence has been perpetrated in the name of God than under any other name. Jesus himself warned against false prophets who would claim his authority as their own.

False prophets are not necessarily insincere. Nothing is that simple. False prophets believe that they are serving a cause which in fact they are betraying. It may sound harsh, but such is the devil's business.

It's hardly surprising. As Shakespeare reminds us, "The devil can cite Scripture for his purpose." Can you think of a more effective way for the devil to work incognito than to show up with a Bible in his hand? Or, as Richard Dudgeon in George Bernard Shaw's *The Devil's Disciple* says, all it takes is "Handel's music and a clergyman to make murder look like piety." In the United States the most effective way to do this is to wrap oneself in the American flag and quote Jesus.

On the other hand, just because a bigot bases his faith upon Jesus, this does not make Jesus' injunction to "Love thine enemy," any less redemptive. In fact, it makes it all the more redemptive, for we are forced, if we wish to remain true to the spirit of Jesus, to love the one who hates even as we abhor his hatred. On the other hand, if we fail in this and hate our enemy, over time we will become like him.

When Bishop Desmond Tutu of South Africa pushed his way through an angry crowd and saved the life of a police informer who had been doused with gasoline and was about to be thrown upon a burning car, he demonstrated with the eloquence of his own action "the need," as he put it, "to use righteous and just means for a righteous and just struggle." Tutu was reminding not only his own people but the whole world of something we somehow find it almost impossible to remember: every time we imitate our enemies, justifying our unethical actions by their unethical behavior, we do the devil's business.

In doing this we have to be particularly careful, for the stakes are high and and we are playing against the devil's strongest hand. Our principal hope is to remember his nature: evil disguised as good.

In Aldous Huxley's *Ape and Essence,* the Arch-Vicar of Belial reminds Huxley's protagonist, Dr. Poole—"whose Liberal-Protestant views about the Devil have been considerably modified during the past few weeks"—that "every conflict over prestige, power or money is a crusade for the Good, the True and the Beautiful."

In the same manner, Milton's Satan is "dark with excessive bright." So too is much if not most of the rhetoric, both religious and political, in our own time. Such words as freedom, truth, goodness, and God are employed to promote every manner of violence. They are printed on the wrapping of every stick of dynamite. They adorn the stated motives of every trader of butter for bombs. Shakespeare put it well in *Hamlet:*

> With devotion's visage
> And pious action we do sugar o'er
> The devil himself.

And yet, if the piety of clergymen and politicians is often indistinguishable, this is not to say, as many liberals do, that there is too much religion in our politics. On the contrary, there is far too little.

The two most graphic definitions of religion to be found anywhere in the Bible are offered by the prophet Micah and by Jesus himself. When asked what is required for the religious life, Micah lists three things: "to do justly, to love mercy and to walk humbly with thy God" (Micah 6:6-8 KJV). In the same spirit, Jesus forsees salvation for those who feed the hungry, clothe the naked, heal the sick, and visit prisoners (Matt. 25:34-36).

Jesus takes Micah's injunction and makes it concrete. Justice, mercy, and humility translate into fairness, kind-ness, and self-giving. One thing worth noting is that neither Micah's nor Jesus' definition of the religious life has any-thing to do with right theology. Nor do they have anything to do with public piety, prayer in schools, or the election, whether political or religious, of God's chosen people.

To combine the two definitions: justice has to do with fairness, mercy with kindness, and, humility with selfless-ness. The irony is that those politicians who most publicly claim to be inspired by the Bible appear spiritually blind when it comes to fairness, deaf in response to the call for kindness, and dumb insofar as any noticeable expression of humility is concerned. In fact, it seems to me that almost all of the religious testimony in recent election years has been singularly lacking in the spirit of fairness, kindness, and certainly humility.

To put this, as Jesus himself did, in more concrete terms, one of the things that is so distressing about the "religious" witness in our politics is that it has little or nothing to say about the poor, hungry, sick, and imprisoned. If political candidates or their supporters want to quote Jesus for their authority, they are probably looking in the wrong place. Jesus does have something important to say, but it is not necessarily what they want to hear.

Neither does the devil want to hear it. After all, his least favorite Scripture is this from the book of Isaiah: "Woe to those who call evil good and good evil" (Isa. 5:20). Small wonder. Less of that all around and the devil's bread and butter would be spoiled.

5. The Devil and the Future

Linehart [entering]: Victory, Your Grace. Victory, complete and classic. An exemplary battle, an epoch-making day. The enemy has lost six thousand men, killed or drowned, the rest are in flight.

The Archbishop: Thanks be to God.

JEAN PAUL SARTRE

No book about the devil would be complete without a chapter on Armageddon. Just to be safe, this one will contain two: first the devil's good news; and then the gospel of Jesus.

Think back to the time when the two of them first met.

The New Testament tells us that after Jesus journeys from Nazareth in Galilee to be baptized by John the Baptist in the river Jordan, the Spirit of God descends upon him like a dove and drives him forth into the wilderness. There he remains with neither food nor shelter, surrounded by wild beasts for forty days. It is here—hungry, tired, and alone—that Jesus is tempted by Satan.

The first temptation is designed to abate Jesus' hunger. A simple miracle is all that it is required. "If thou be the Son of God, command that these stones be made bread," Satan suggests. To which Jesus replies, "It is written, man shall not live by bread alone, but by every word that proceedeth out of the mouth of God."

Having once been thwarted, Satan tries a second ploy. Where hunger had failed, surely pride—designed by the devil to come before a fall—would conquer Jesus' resistance and bring him into the devil's service. So the devil takes Jesus to Jerusalem and sets him on the pinnacle of the temple mount. "If thou be the Son of God," Satan says to Jesus, "cast thyself down; for it is written, he shall give his angels charge concerning thee: and in their hands they shall bear thee up, lest at any time thou dash thy foot against a stone." And indeed, Satan would have saved Jesus. An angel still, though fallen, the prince of the power of the air, he would have swept Jesus up and settled him down gently beyond the gravestones in the valley below. But again Jesus demurs: "Thou shalt not tempt the Lord thy God," he says.

Where hunger and pride had failed, surely power would succeed. No one knew the lure of power better than Satan. As he understood so well, power is irresistible, and as the god of this world it was his to offer. So he takes Jesus up to a high mountain and shows him all the kingdoms of the world in a moment of time. "All this power will I give thee, and the glory of them," Satan promises, "for that is delivered unto me; and to whomsoever I will I give it. If thou therefore wilt worship me, all shall be thine." To which Jesus replies, "Get thee hence, Satan: for it is written, thou shalt worship the Lord thy God, and Him only shalt thou serve." And so the devil departs from Jesus, "but only for a season" (Matt. 4:1-11 KJV).

Jesus was crucified some three years later. As Satan continues to range over the earth from end to end, each succeeding generation of Christians confidently prophesies Jesus' imminent return for the final defense of his title. The promotional teasers announcing this event are posted in the Book of Revelation: that "famous book," to quote Bierce, "in which St. John the Divine concealed all that he knew, [while] the revealing is done by the commentators, who know nothing." It is by far the devil's favorite book in all the Bible, and, the last to make it into the canon.

There are good reasons for the devil's fondness for this strange apocalyptic tract. For one thing, nothing pleases the devil more than for people to engage with earnest solemnity in the interpretation of cosmic runes. Which is simply to say that were they not so innocuous the devil would absolutely thrive on astrologers.

We have more able servants, however. In our own generation, for instance, more than 15 million people have read *The Late Great Planet Earth,* Hal Lindsey's harrowing account of the coming last days. As I remember all too well as a student preparing for my doctoral exams, dozens of such works, many far superior in their title to scholarship, were written predicting that the end of the world would occur just at the turn of the last millennium.

But where others have failed, who are we not to succeed? And so, undaunted, Mr. Lindsey forges ahead, identifying the names and numbers of all the players. His chapter titles tell the story: "Russia Is a Gog," or "Sheik to Sheik," not to mention "The Yellow Peril."

As Lindsey reminds us, among the hallmarks that will guarantee Christ's official and fully authorized return to earth are that it will be visible and physical; sudden and startling; and with violent judgment. Can you think of any better or more textually apt fulfillment of John's prophecy than the physical, sudden, startling, and violent destruction of the planet in nuclear war? The devil's all for it. In fact, it's number one on his own agenda. He calls it "The Rapture."

Short of this, the devil will settle for Utopia. To get a taste of what he means, let's turn to another story that

reports the events that follow upon Christ's return, Ivan
Karamazov's "The Grand Inquisitor" from Dostoevsky's *The
Brothers Karamazov.*

It takes place fifteen centuries after Jesus' first encounter
with the devil and is set in Spain during the height of the
Inquisition. History is filled with little Armageddons, past,
present, and future, and on this occasion Jesus "wanted to
come only for a moment to visit His children and He chose
to appear where the fires were crackling under the heretics."

Jesus arrives in the sunbaked city of Seville one day
after nearly a hundred heretics had been torched for the
greater glory of God. This was done by order of the Cardinal, the Grand Inquisitor. Naturally, it took place before
the royalty and entire population of this great city.

At first Jesus moves unobserved through the crowd; but,
though he says nothing, one by one the people recognize
him and are drawn to him as if by an irresistible force.
That force is love. It burns in his heart. Light, understanding, and spiritual power flow from him with healing strength.
But just as Jesus pauses near the steps of the cathedral
erected in his name, the Cardinal himself appears, crossing
the cathedral square, his face dark with anger. He points
his finger at Jesus and calls upon his guards to seize him
at once and lock him away. The Cardinal's power is so great
that the people, even those who recognize Jesus, don't
protest.

When the Grand Inquisitor visits Jesus in his cell later
that evening, Jesus says nothing. Only the Cardinal speaks.
"You? Is it really You?" he asks. "Why did You come here,
to interfere and make things difficult for us? . . . I don't
know whether You are really He or just a likeness of him,
but no later than tomorrow I shall pronounce You the

wickedest of all heretics and sentence You to be burned at the stake." His motives, of course, are good: to ensure human happiness. "When You were on earth, . . . didn't You often tell people that You wanted to make them free? That business cost us a great deal. . . . For fifteen hundred years we were pestered by that notion of freedom, but in the end we succeeded in getting rid of it. People today are convinced that they are freer than they have ever been, although over the centuries they themselves brought us their freedom and put it meekly at our feet." Thus did the Church give happiness to humankind.

Not unlike the paradise promised at the end of the Book of Revelation, what we have here is a return to Eden. Whereas Adam and Eve in exercising their freedom disobeyed God and fell from grace, here a perfect society has been created where freedom no longer is a problem, or at least will be no problem, as soon as all the heretics, including Jesus, are burned.

As the Grand Inquisitor reminds him, long ago when tempted by the devil—"the wise and dreaded spirit of self-destruction and non-existence"—Jesus too had an opportunity to usher in a new age of perfect obedience. "Man has no more pressing, agonizing need than the need to find someone to whom he can hand over as quickly as possible the gift of freedom with which the poor wretch comes into the world." By yielding to temptation, Jesus "would have fulfilled man's greatest need on earth. That is, the need to find someone to worship, someone who can relieve him of the burden of his conscience, thus enabling him finally to unite into a harmonious ant-hill where there are no dissenting voices."

But here again Jesus failed.

"What came of it?" the Grand Inquisitor asks. "Instead of seizing men's freedom, You gave them even more of it! Have You forgotten that peace, and even death, is more attractive to man than the freedom of choice that derives from the knowledge of good and evil?"

But all was not lost, for where Jesus was unwilling to lead the church was eager to follow. "We have corrected Your work and have now founded it on *miracle, mystery,* and *authority*. And men rejoice at being led like cattle again, with the terrible gift of freedom that brought them so much suffering removed from them." Just the devil's cup of tea: religion without questions or tears.

By now there is absolutely no question as to who is in charge. The Grand Inquisitor serves the devil in Christ's name. "How could I expect to hide our secret from You?" he asks. "But perhaps You want to hear it from my own lips? Listen, then: we are not with You, we are with *him*—and that is our secret, our mystery!"

Consider it from the devil's perspective. It's heaven on earth. After all, having fallen himself, he knows as well as anyone how costly freedom can be. And short of nuclear annihilation, a return to Eden is the next best thing, so long as the devil is in charge and not God. It's really quite simple. Free choice is taken away, the fall reversed, the knowledge of good and evil returned to the authorities, and everyone else left free to sin in little ways and with a clear conscience. "Everyone will be happy," the Grand Inquisitor tells Jesus, "all the millions of beings, with the exception of the hundred thousand men who are called upon to rule over them. For only we, the keepers of the secret, will be unhappy. There will be millions upon millions of happy babes and one hundred thousand sufferers who have accepted the burden of the knowledge of good and evil."

The devil, of course, is a Utopian, always dreaming of systems so perfect such as this one devised by the church of the Grand Inquisitor. But since the past can't always be counted on to deliver, the devil is also a futurist. Short of nuclear Armageddon, which for him would represent the ideal "final solution" to all our problems, there are any number of attractive short-term alternatives.

If you study them carefully, you will discover that each of the devil's systems, not unlike that of his servant the Grand Inquisitor, depends to one degree or another upon the curtailment of freedom. Though our propensity already is to squander whatever freedom we possess in ways that bind us to the tyranny either of our own petty appetites or of the appetites of those in power—in church, business, or state—the devil realizes that so long as we retain even the slightest vestige of true freedom, we are capable of investing it in things that will ennoble us and serve the commonweal. Finally, though the odds are long, the devil also knows that if enough of us are awakened to act upon our freedom and to act with love, we may even manage to defuse the instruments we have built for own destruction.

But as it stands right now, the devil has things in fairly good control. As the Arch-Vicar of Belial says in Huxley's *Ape and Essence,* "I tell you, my dear sir, an undevout historian is mad. The longer you study modern history, the more evidence you find of Belial's guiding Hand."

Huxley's novel is the tale of the Grand Inquisitor set in the future. Here the devil's two most effective tools are progress and nationalism. Citing Karl Marx's statement that "Force is the midwife of Progress," Huxley points out that progress is also the midwife of force. Technological progress provides us with the satanic instruments of mass destruction, while the myth of political and moral superiority serves as an idolatrous pretext for endlessly expanding our arsenals. As the Arch-Vicar says, "Utopia lies just ahead. . . . Since ideal ends justify the most abominable means, it is your privilege and duty to rob, swindle, torture, enslave and murder all those who, in your opinion (which is, by definition, infallible), obstruct the onward march to the earthly paradise."

We can always point to the Soviets. They have written the book on this sort of thing. Which is not say that we haven't studied it carefully.

One small but telling illustration. In 1975 the Senate Intelligence Committee, chaired by my father, Frank Church, uncovered evidence of five unsuccessful CIA-sponsored assassination plots against foreign leaders. In issuing his report Church wrote, "The United States must not adopt the tactics of the enemy. Means are as important as ends. Crisis makes it tempting to ignore the wise restraints that make men free; but each time we do so, each time the means we use are wrong, our inner strength, the strength which makes us free, is lessened."

Elsewhere he said, speaking of the founders of our country, "They acted on their faith, not their fear. They did not believe in fighting fire with fire; crime with crime; evil with evil; or delinquency by becoming delinquents. . . . They knew that the only way to escape a closed society was to accept the risk of living in an open one."

One result of Senator Church's report was the passage of a law prohibiting the United States, through any branch of its government, from future involvement in political assassination. But in response to the feeling of outrage and helplessness that accompanied the TWA hijacking which led to death of one American and the detainment of thirty-nine others in Beirut in June 1985, this law was suddenly in jeopardy. It turns out that our principles are inconvenient in a world where terrorism and lawlessness exist. Too often, we are frustrated by our inability to exact revenge.

But we forget one thing. If, as they are often taught, instant bliss is the reward for death in a holy cause, religious zealots—whether terrorist, holy innocent, or both—are delighted to don the martyr's crown. And even if they don't win a free ride to heaven, here on earth their holy cause will surely be advanced. For as one early church father, Tertullian, reminded the Romans in his own day, "the blood of the martyrs is the seed of the church."

Senator Church's law against assassination was only one potential sacrifice to be burned on the altar of the "new patriotism" here in the United States. In the same year of our Lord 1985, with devilish irony just before the July 4th recess, the following legislation was offered before Congress: one amendment to the Defense authorization bill that would legalize the assassination of terrorists; another that would permit random polygraphing of millions of Americans employed by the Pentagon and defense contractors; and a third that would restore the death penalty for peacetime espionage.

It seems the devil has a rapt audience whenever he points out how tough it is to be an American these days. And he's right—openness is often inconvenient.

Conservative philosopher Sidney Hook laments "how fragile a self-governing democratic society is. . . . For its very own rationale encourages a constant critical approach that its enemies can exploit to weaken it." In his book *How Democracies Perish,* Jean-François Revel warns that not only is a democracy "not basically structured to defend itself against outside enemies . . . , [but also] democracy faces an internal enemy whose right to exist is written into the law itself." We are also told time and again that the U.S. press is insufficiently patriotic, insufficiently anti-Soviet, and too objective. Such critics would feel right at home in the Soviet Union, where they rewrite history and filter current events through a red lens as suits their ideological taste.

New Republic columnist Michael Kinsley sums up the "new patriotism" and its accompanying argument in favor of a new *Realpolitik* in these words: "Nations like America are too decent and humanitarian for our own damn good." He goes on to add, "I wish that the putative defenders of American liberty and democracy would show a bit more enthusiasm for these fine things. Instead, they criticize America's openness, its idealism, its raucous dissent as unsuitable to this cold world."

One thing is for sure: idealism, openness, and raucous dissent are insults to the devil and his plans for us. Still, he is patient. He knows how easily we human beings can convince ourselves to do the wrong thing for the right reason. And, to promote his own cause in this regard, he has two things working for him. One is that, over time, we become very like the enemies we choose for ourselves. And the other is that, unconscious of the good in our enemies and terrified by their evil, we eventually will become like them at their worst.

But even without enemies to imitate, the devil knows that we are eminently capable on our own of fashioning noble pretexts to rationalize the destruction of ourselves, one another, and the world. The Eternal Malcontent, as Friedrich Nietzsche called the devil, is "Man's best force," representing our progressive, inquisitive nature, which will not permit us to settle for lesser achievement, but urges us on to higher and nobler aims.

Indeed. As in Upton Sinclair's play *Hell*, where the devil exults:

> Progress, my lords! System and science combined!
> Once men were worms, they crawled upon the ground,
> Stung one another into misery;
> Now they have wings, they imitate the wasps.

Like Nietzsche, Ivan Karamazov was a modern man. He perceived the evil of the church, namely, that it was bitten by the tremendous and self-serving temptation to crucify again and again the very one in whose name it was established. But like most of us, he was blind in the other eye. Here, filtered through his double, the devil, is Ivan's "Utopian" vision of the future.

Once every member of the human race discards the idea of God (and I believe that such an era will come, like some new geological age), the old world-view will collapse by itself without recourse to cannibalism. And the first thing to disintegrate will be the old morality, for everything will be new and different. Men will unite their efforts to get everything out of life that it can offer them, but only for joy and happiness in this world. Man will be exalted spiritually with a divine, titanic pride and the man-god will come into being. Extending his conquest over nature beyond all bounds through his will and his science, man will constantly experience such great joy that it will replace for him his former anticipation of the pleasures that await him in heaven.

It seems that if the devil doesn't catch us fleeing from

the present to capture some lost, presumed Arcadia, he catches us advancing into the future, running from all restraints that have bound us in the past. In fact, when it comes to every "-ology" and "-ism" devised by humankind, as Reinhold Niebuhr reminds us, we are "constantly tempted to forget the finiteness of [our] cultures and civilisation and to pretend a finality for them which they do not have. Every civilisation and every culture is thus a Tower of Babel."

Aldous Huxley's Arch-Vicar takes a swig from his bottle.

Even without the atomic bomb, Belial could have achieved all His purposes. A little more slowly, perhaps, but just as surely, men would have destroyed themselves by destroying the world they lived in. . . . Fouling the rivers, killing off the wild animals, destroying the forests, washing the topsoil into the sea, burning up an ocean of petroleum, squandering the minerals it had taken the whole of geological time to deposit. An orgy of criminal imbecility. And they called it Progress.

Huxley was writing in 1948, the year I was born. He set his novel in 2108. The devil is way ahead of schedule.

Since idolatry is the devil's specialty and deceit his manner, in his plans for our future, religion plays—as it does in Dostoevski's and Huxley's tales—the central role.

In the Book of Revelation the white horse of the apocalypse represents counterfeit religion, its rider wearing a crown of victory and holding a bow of great destruction in his hand. Christ also appears in the Book of Revelation crowned and mounted on a white charger descending from the clouds to claim victory in the final battle. Just try to tell the two of them apart.

In his strange prophetic prose poem "Jerusalem," William Blake writes that, "Man must and will have Some

Religion. If he has not the Religion of Jesus, he will have the Religion of Satan, ... calling the Prince of this World, God, and destroying all who do not worship Satan under the Name of God." Blake targets two groups, the religious fundamentalists and the religious liberals of his own day. As to the former, he says, "Every Religion that Preaches Vengeance for Sin is the Religion of the Enemy and Avenger and not of the Forgiver of Sin, and their God is Satan, Named by the Divine Name." As to the latter, "Your Religion, O Deists ... is the Worship of the God of this World by the means of what you call Natural Religion and Natural Philosophy, and of Natural Morality, or Self-Righteousness, the Selfish Virtues of the Natural Heart."

The devil will tell us that this doesn't begin to cover all the bases, but at least it gives two major groups one another to damn. As the devil will also tell us, so long as we continue to raise the banner of our own goodness in every battle we wage against the evil of others, his position in the future will be assured. Whatever the outcome, he will always win.

When Ivan Karamazov's brother Alyosha asks how he intends to conclude his story of the Grand Inquisitor and Jesus, Ivan replies, "The Grand Inquisitor falls silent and waits for some time for the prisoner to answer." The old man longs to hear Jesus say something, but instead Jesus suddenly arises and goes over to the tough old Cardinal and kisses him gently. That is the Christ's only response.

And at the end of *Ape and Essence,* Dr. Poole fashions this simple protest against the rule of Belial, where not only freedom but love too is proscribed. "If we feel and think and do the right thing, He can't hurt us," Poole tells the woman he's with. "But what *is* the right thing?" she asks. For a second or two he smiles at her without speaking. "Here and now," he says at last, "the right thing is *this*." He slips an arm about her shoulders and draws her toward him.

6. Jesus and the Future

Put on the whole armor of God, that you may be able to stand against
the wiles of the devil. For we are not contending against flesh and blood,
but against the principalities, against the powers, against the world rulers
of this present darkness, against the spiritual hosts of wickedness in the
heavenly places.

ST. PAUL (EPH.6,11–12)

I don't think I've mentioned how much the devil loves
pollsters. It's just one of his little sins, but he almost never
fails to find something in a poll that prompts him to admire
his own handiwork.

One of the devil's favorite polls is the one on religion
periodically sponsored by the Gallup organization. Take,
for instance, the results of a recent Gallup poll on Jesus.
Among the findings: ¾ of the 1,500 Americans polled believe that Jesus is alive in heaven; 62 percent believe that
he will return to earth; 71 percent say they are deepening
their personal relationship with Jesus; and yet, when it
comes to exploring just how deep that relationship goes, it
turns out that nearly 60 percent of those questioned do not
even know that Jesus delivered the Sermon on the Mount.
No matter, nine out of ten still say that they have been
influenced by Jesus as a moral and ethical teacher. Where
they get their information is a bit of a mystery. When asked
to name the four Gospels, 43 percent of the 1,500 people
who were questioned were not able to name a single one.

It is no different in Europe. I heard over the radio
recently of a poll conducted in the Common Market countries.

Evidently, upon being asked who Jesus is, the majority of those who called themselves atheists answered that Jesus is the Son of God.

As the devil will delight in demonstrating to all those rational-minded folks who are tempted in the direction of unbelief, religion defies all logic. This is why religious proofs for the existence of God or Jesus as Messiah are so often uncompelling to anyone who is not already convinced.

It reminds me of the story of the researcher who trained a flea to jump over his finger on the shouted command, "Jump!" After the flea had become proficient, the researcher, in the interests of science, removed its front legs. The flea was still able to obey the command and jumped almost as nimbly as before. After its middle legs were removed, with some difficulty the little fellow mastered the trick once again. But when its rear legs were removed, the flea made no response to the shouted command. Dutifully, the researcher entered into his notebook this conclusion: "When you cut all the legs off a flea, it becomes deaf."

But, skeptics, beware.

The Greek philosopher Aristotle is the great-grandfather of all those who pride themselves on their critical faculties, their objectivity, their impeccable logic. Among other things, Aristotle discovered the law of the excluded middle: something cannot be true and false at the same time. For instance, a day cannot be both hot and cold, nor can we be successful if we are failures. It makes sense, but there is one problem. When it comes to religion, none of this is true.

To direct us, many religious signs—not signs that explain, but signs that illumine—point us clearly beyond logic and into the realm of paradox. Paradox means "contrary to right opinion." Our word dogma stems from the same Greek root. Dogma (right teaching) and paradox (that which flies in the face of right teaching) are opposites.

For instance, in writings as far-flung as the gospel of Jesus and the Tao of Lao-tse, the last are first, the rich are poor, and the person who loses his life saves it. The Buddha and St. Francis give up their inherited wealth and position and find enlightenment; they empty themselves and are filled. Jesus teaches that only the sinner—the outcast Samaritan, the prodigal son—stands much of a chance of being saved. He answers hate with love and gains his final victory on the cross. And before he dies, to whom does he pass on his mantle? It is to Peter: Peter who falls asleep when Jesus asks him to stand guard as he prays; Peter who betrays his teacher three times because of his fears; Peter the weak; Peter the failure; Peter the rock upon whom Christ builds his church.

Paradox upon paradox.

It should therefore come as no surprise that Jesus, even as he predicts the end of the world, at the same time teaches us how to save it.

For years the fact that Jesus believed that the world was about to end has proved an embarrassment to liberal Christians. We gloss over passages like the one in Matthew 16:27–28 where Jesus says to his disciples that soon "the Son of man shall come in the glory of his Father with his angels; and then shall he reward every man according to his works. Verily I say unto you, there be some standing here, which shall not taste of death, till they see the Son of man coming in his kingdom."

In fact, such passages as this have posed a problem not only for liberal Christians, but for Christians of many different persuasions.

The truth is, Jesus was wrong. Despite his expectation, the end of the world was not at hand. Despite his prediction, the kingdom did not come. Notwithstanding the self-centered assurances of those who ardently believe that when Jesus was talking about the coming of the kingdom two thousand years ago, he was actually predicting that the kingdom would come not in his disciples' lifetime but hundreds of years later in their own, the hard fact remains. For two millennia Christians have been preaching a gospel that is founded upon a mistaken view of history.

Ironically, it was a liberal interpreter who brought this question to the forefront of biblical scholarship. In 1906 Albert Schweitzer wrote a book entitled *The Quest of the Historical Jesus.* It revolutionized the debate over Jesus and his teachings.

Schweitzer argued that Jesus' preaching centered almost entirely upon preparing his disciples for the imminent coming of the kingdom of God. Accordingly, the only way to understand Jesus' message was to remember the time-frame in which it was to apply. The ethical teaching of Jesus was not presented as a set of timeless truths to guide the moral life of Christians for generations to come. Instead, he confronted his own generation with an eleventh-hour call for repentance. Forget the niceties of the law, he said. Waste no time on theological hair-splitting, for the end is at hand. Only two commandments matter any more, love of God and love of neighbor. To honor them, absolute and immediate repentance is required. Only those who are morally renewed and transformed will have a place in the coming kingdom.

Jesus contributed to the history of ethics such radical notions as the love of enemies; and, from his own Jewish tradition, he recovered an oft-forgotten truth, the futility of self-righteousness. He surrounded himself with whores and tax collectors—remember the taxes were 80 percent in Judea at the time and collectors' profits came off the top— with pariahs, therefore, outcasts and renegades.

All those who were vested in the world, whether for wealth, sensual gratification, or power, he accounted as almost hopelessly lost. There was time, just barely, for repentance and forgiveness, but no time whatsoever for self-righteousness and pride.

Albert Schweitzer called it interim ethics, or an "ethic for the interim" between Jesus' proclamation and the dawning of the new age. To translate this into the context of our own times, it has nothing to do with prayer in the public schools, tuition tax credits, the putative evil of homosexuality, or the number of the beast. There was no time for any of that. Believing that the end of the world was at hand, Jesus told his disciples that they would be hard enough pressed to remove the beam from their own eye, never mind the mote in their neighbor's. He told them to save their stones of judgment for themselves. Schweitzer himself puts it this way: "The good conscience is an invention of the devil."

Today, if the end of the world is at hand, it is not because the kingdom prophesied by Jesus is coming. Rather, it is because we have it within our own power for the first time in history to blow ourselves to kingdom come. And yet, however different from the end that Jesus envisioned, and however far removed from the theological presuppositions of his own gospel, is it not possible that because of this Jesus' ethical teachings are even more relevant now that the end of the world may truly be at hand than they were in his own day?

Think of what this radical gospel, especially the stress it places upon interim ethics, might mean for us. Powered by the expectation that the world would end in his followers' lifetimes, Jesus' message was appropriately blunt, absolute, and unadorned. He called upon his disciples to repent; to transform their lives according to the dual commandment of love to God and love to neighbor; and to do this at once, not tomorrow, for tomorrow might be too late.

Look at it from our perspective. So long as we hold it in our power to destroy ourselves and one another in an unthinkable but ever more likely apocalypse, the love commandment again becomes, perhaps as never before, a moral imperative. In fact, nuclear disarmament and the love commandment are almost interchangeable.

On the other hand Jesus may have demanded more than human nature will allow. For who is this neighbor that Jesus says we must love now that the world is about to end? Try the Grand Inquisitor. Kiss him on the cheek. Try the premier of the Soviet Union or the president of the United States, each reviewing contingency plans for our mutual annihilation. Try the television evangelist condemning you to hell if you don't accept his political platform for the coming election. Perhaps even more difficult, try your ex-husband, or the person who just fired you from your job, or even your nettlesome next-door neighbor!

Especially if the end of the world is at hand, and if Jesus' teachings have any bearing upon our situation, we have no time left to hate these people. Or even, by responding in negative ways, to protect ourselves from them. All we have time for is a change of heart. All we have time for is love.

Albert Schweitzer too was an idealist. In his later books,

and especially in the witness of his life, Dr. Schweitzer found ways to translate Jesus' message for his own time. "In Jesus Christ, God is manifested as Will of Love," Schweitzer wrote. "Men are to be gripped by God's will of love, and must help to carry out that will in this world, in small things as in great things, in saving as in pardoning." Schweitzer further characterized this calling as "active self-devotion to others, as the philosophy and ethic of reverence for life; and as the ethic or religion of love."

In his own time, of course, not too many people listened to Jesus. Those who did were reviled both by the religious establishment and by skeptics and unbelievers, any of whom could point out, among other things, that Jesus' prophecy that the world was about to end did not come true. But today, to cite yet another of the devil's favorite polls, nearly half of the people in this country believe that the world will end in their own lifetime. Many of these same people cast their ballots for candidates for whom missiles are "peace-keepers" and whose fearful ideology—founded on fear and inspiring fear—dramatically undercuts the diminishing chances for meaningful negotiations to keep the peace. It may not make sense to us, but it does to the devil.

When considering Jesus' ethics for our own age there are other things to remember. First, when Jesus was talking about the future, he had his eye on the present. With the end imminent, the time-frame narrowed. The future was no longer some distant tomorrow, but a thief in the night of this very day. Second, interim ethics were not only here and now, but one on one. Jesus didn't say, "Love your neighbors as yourself"; he said, "Love your *neighbor* as yourself." (Matt. 22:39). We shall see that the two are not the same, not at all. Third, Jesus' teachings are not confirmed by his triumph. They are confirmed by his death on the cross.

Let's take each of these in turn.

First, the future. When Jesus was speaking of the future, he was talking about the kingdom. He meant two different things by this. On the one hand, the kingdom was yet to come; on the other, it had already arrived.

These two concepts are not as far apart as they may seem. Remember, the time-frame has narrowed. The end of the world is at hand. A taste of heaven today might tonight be a feast forever—which is simply to say that the future is at work in Jesus' teaching, but almost wholly in present tense. Today and tonight, not tomorrow.

The key to interim ethics is to live in the present as if one were already living in the kingdom. Each of our decisions becomes an ultimate decision, one upon which judgment is weighed. For all practical purposes, the future disappears.

This is where Jesus and the devil part company. The future that Jesus was speaking about and that in which the devil delights are mirror images of one another. For Jesus the future dimension is one of eternal fullness; for the devil it is a dimension of eternal emptiness. For Jesus it invests the present with ultimate meaning; for the devil it transfers meaning outside of the present and leaves us in a hollow state of incompletion, of longing. For Jesus it is heaven; for the devil it is hell.

Speaking of the devil's sort of future, C.S. Lewis wrote that making people live in the future "inflames hope and fear."

The future is, of all things, the thing *least like* eternity. It is the most completely temporal part of time—for the past is frozen and no longer flows, and the present is all lit up with eternal rays. Hence the encouragement we have given to all those schemes of thought such as Creative Evolution, Scientific Humanism, or Communism, which fix men's affections on the future, on the very core of temporality. Nearly all vices are rooted in the future. Gratitude looks to the past and love to the present; fear, avarice, lust and ambition look ahead."

In Dante's *Inferno,* one distinguishing feature of the damned is that, although they can see the future, they are unable to see the present. This is true of all but the prophets. In the eighth circle of Hell, where Dante finds Diviners, Astrologers, and Magicians, all of them have their heads turned backward. They can see neither present nor future, only the past.

Which leads us to love. What is missing in their lives and deaths is love. Shared love can only take place in the present. In each perfect act of love—not love in the abstract but earthy love—the realm of God is entered, the past redeemed, and, for a blessed moment, the devil put to rout.

You see, love is not something that we offer to others, but to another. To paraphrase the Talmud, we save ourselves and the world one neighbor at a time. It is frustrating, of course. Recognizing the enormity of the world's problems—the problems of hunger and war and injustice—it is hard to justify rolling up our sleeves and pitching in wherever it is we happen to be just to make one single life a little better. It's more than hard. In fact, it appears so defeating that any effort seems absurd.

The devil, on the other hand, doesn't deal in nitty gritty, but almost entirely in abstraction. That is one of the reasons that he is so fond of the arms race. In a single atomic submarine we carry atomic megatonage six times greater than that of all the bombs exploded during World War II.

Just try to fathom it. It is almost impossible to do. In our collective arsenals we and the Soviets are stocked to deliver thousands of times as much devastation as we were able to muster then, fire power sufficient to destroy one another and the entire planet as well several times over.

The devil will tell us that there is almost nothing we can do about any of this. He will also tell us that we'd better watch out, for our enemies are after us. And then he will sing the devil's chant from Upton Sinclair's play, *Hell*.

> For all the booboisie of Earth to sing;
> Preparedness is Safety—meaning this,
> Each man is safe in cheerful certainty
> That he can cut his neighbor's throat the first.

Or, as Mammon exults in taking over the earth's corporate empires and turning them to his own devices.

> It's the guns!
> That shall not cease again upon the Earth
> Till all mankind has blown itself to Hell!
> Behold our enginery!

Another way in which the devil deals in abstraction is when he helps us to justify continuing our arms buildup at the expense of social programs. We are not talking here about taking food off the Smiths' family table. We are talking about "the poor," "the homeless," and "the hungry." Or when funds are cut for family planning, we are not talking about Sally Jones. We are talking about "unwed mothers." As William F. May writes, "Sins against the needy are, in an important sense, the exact opposite of those against the enemy. The enemy occupies the center of attention. But the needy, at the other extreme, barely exists."

The devil, of course, is into success. Jesus was not. This should give those of us with little hope at least a bit of courage. Without daring to fail, or being given the opportunity to fail, how could Jesus ever have succeeded to the extent that he did?

Take the events leading up to his Crucifixion. How easily things could have turned out differently.

Pilate, it seems, was a man of some conscience. He was uncomfortable handing Jesus over to be crucified. For one thing, it was far from clear that Jesus had done any wrong. He certainly had broken no laws of the state. As long as Jesus continued to exhort his followers to give unto Caesar what was Caesar's, there could be no harm in countenancing his continued presence.

In Pilate's opinion, Jesus was nothing more than a minor Jewish prophet and wonderworker. There were many such figures in Judea. They were not Pilate's kind of people. He was a rational man, a good liberal. He had no use for religious fanatics, though Jesus, he had to admit, was interesting. Imagine, the man wouldn't say a word in his own behalf. Seemingly, he was unconcerned about his fate. This appealed to Pilate's Stoic sensibilities. Not only that, but there was also the question of Pilate's wife. Had she not written him a note while he was sitting in judgment upon Jesus, imploring him in these words: "Let there be nothing between you and this just man; for I have suffered much today because of a dream about him" (Matt.27:19).

But Pilate was a rational man. He didn't put too much stock in dreams. On the other hand, he knew enough not to dismiss them entirely. Nor was he one to cross his wife lightly. And so he sat. And he asked questions. And he listened as the case against Jesus was presented, taking into account the Sanhderin, especially the Sadducees, who seemed most threatened by the competition Jesus offered. Pilate had to admit that something would be gained by giving in to them. But he just could not bring himself to do it.

"Enough," he finally said. "Even my wife has suffered from your foolishness. And this man, Jesus, goodness knows, has suffered enough. He does not threaten Rome. It is not he who spawns civil unrest in Judea. The law of Rome protects those who do no wrong. We need peace, not another martyr. I will be truly innocent of the blood of this man. I keep Barabbas. I give you Jesus. He can go. He can preach. He can practice his healing throughout Judea. The power of Rome will go with him and protect him. Jesus will suffer no more."

So it was that Jesus continued to teach in parables and to minister to the sick. His ethical message remained as before, the message of the progressive rabbis of his day, except for one, distinctive, radical insight: "Love your enemies. Forgive them. Do good to those who persecute you."

But no one dared to be Jesus' enemy, at least not openly. And no one persecuted him, for on Pilate's instruction the legions of Rome watched over him and made sure that he came to no harm. He was admired, even revered by some. But most regarded him as an amiable eccentric who preached in pious hyperbole about loving hypothetical enemies and praying for mythical persecutors.

Jesus died of old age in Nazareth in his carpentry shop, slumped across a wooden workbench. The night before he died, when at supper with his aging followers, he turned to the one whom he had forgiven the most and loved the most and said to him, "Judas, let me tell you. Pilate's vow holds me prisoner, even as his justice gives me joy. I came to usher in the Kingdom of God, to create it here on earth. Creation is composed of both joy and suffering. The pains of this new and wondrous birth have been denied me. The world is little changed for all my years of teaching. I must go to my Father having drunk the bitterest cup of all."

None of this happened, of course. But perhaps we can learn from what didn't happen something about what did.

Jesus entered Jerusalem festively, leading a band of his followers, people who believed that he was the promised messiah. Within a week he had been betrayed by one of his disciples, brought before Pilate, sentenced, and crucified. His followers disbanded. Many, in fear for their own lives, went into hiding. His chief disciple, Peter, forswore him three times rather than admitting to any knowledge of him.

This is certainly not the way the story was supposed to turn out. By ancient tradition the promised messiah, scion of David, King of the Jews, would march triumphantly into Jerusalem to be crowned. This was the expectation of many of Jesus' followers. The problem is, their expectation had nothing whatsoever to do with Jesus' gospel.

Empty yourself and be filled. That was the essence of his message. *Lose your life and find new life. Dare to suffer and be part of a new creation.* Paradox upon paradox. *The kingdom of God is in a mustard seed,* the smallest and least portentous of all seeds; *riches are impediments to salvation; all the knowledge of the scribes, all the logic of the Pharisees, and all the pretense of the Sadducees is a sham—it accounts for nothing.* If Jesus is right, it is small wonder that we tend to mistake God for the devil and the devil for God. Each is likely to pop up where we would expect to find the other.

And yet the two could not be more different. One key to the difference is that the devil's good news celebrates taking through selfish love. Jesus' gospel—the very opposite—celebrates giving through sacrificial love.

Loving one's enemy is surely a kind of sacrificial love. To love an enemy, we must sacrifice our pride. We must sacrifice our sense of entitlement, and all the pleasures that go into salving a wounded ego with vengefulness, bitterness, and hate.

Forgiveness too requires sacrifice. Fully to forgive, we must sacrifice self-righteousness. We must sacrifice our preoccupation with having been wronged. And we must sacrifice the advantage of holding another in our debt.

The word sacrifice means "to render sacred."

Jesus' teachings and especially his parables are filled with this message. But it is a hard and radical message, and his disciples did not begin to understand what he was saying to them. As a matter of fact, if you reread the Gospels you will discover that they are filled with Jesus' voiced frustration at his own disciples' inability to apprehend the deeper meaning of his words.

For instance, many before him had preached that one must love one's neighbor as oneself. But Jesus redefined the word neighbor. It is this that confounded his disciples. To cast his message in modern terms, our neighbors are the Russians. Our neighbors are the winos and bag ladies, even those who hurl curses at us when we try to help them. Our neighbor is the man who betrayed our trust.

Our neighbor is the lover who left us without just cause. It is no wonder that this message eluded Jesus' disciples— not only those who walked with him, but also those who have followed in his name.

If the essence of Jesus' gospel is summed up anywhere, it is in his agony on the cross: suffering; self-sacrifice; forgiving one's enemies; and submitting to the mysterious, inscrutable, and often paradoxical will of God. Listen to his dying words. "I thirst," he said. "It is finished" (John 19:28, 30). "Father, forgive them; for they know not what they do" (Luke 23:34). "Into thy hands I commit my spirit" (Luke 23:46). Take away the passion and there is no triumph. There is no new creation.

The issue here is not the physical resurrection of Jesus. The affirmation and triumph of Jesus' gospel come during the passion itself. The resurrection is simply the fruit of that passion, the symbol of its integrity. This is true whether one takes the Gospel accounts literally or figuratively. In either case, the message remains the same. It is a message founded on suffering (the suffering of Jesus) and grounded in failure (in this case not the failure of Jesus, but the failure of Pilate and the failure of Judas and the failure of Peter).

Pilate tries to wash his hands clean of his failure. That points to the lesson. Judas tries to cash in on his failure. That also points to the lesson. Peter begs forgiveness for his failure. And he is forgiven. The suffering Christ that was in Jesus on the Cross is born again in Peter, who has learned the lesson of Easter through his ignominy and his tears. The Kingdom of God that was within Jesus reigns now, resurrected, in Peter's heart.

Of course we have cut our teeth on a radically different

gospel, the devil's good news! Put in a nutshell, nothing succeeds like success, with its evident corollary, failure is to be avoided. Not that we do avoid it. But, like Judas and even more like Pilate, we tend to finesse it. We tend to blame our suffering on others and make excuses for our failures. Most pathetic of all, we tend to avoid situations in which we might place ourselves at risk: not daring to speak out when justice is left undone; not daring to formulate convictions so sound that we will be inconvenienced should we attempt to live by them; not daring to assume personal responsibility; and, most important of all, not daring to probe our life's meaning, this for fear we might discover just what it would take to make our lives worth living and worth dying for.

The problem is simple. One way or another, we are always in danger of finding out the truth about ourselves. And when we do, or even begin to get a glimmering of it, we are met with the demand that we must change. The devil will dissuade us, for just think of what this might mean. It likely means emptying ourselves before we can be filled, perhaps in a sense even losing our lives before they can be found; and, short of this, it surely means giving up a modicum of comfort, convenience, and security.

Imagine that you and I were brought before the tribunal of meaning and purpose, of truth and conscience, of love. Let's ask ourselves, as if it really did make a difference: Are we in any danger of being convicted of self-sacrifice, or heartfelt forgiveness, or a sufficient generosity of spirit that we may be said truly to love our neighbor as ourself? And if convicted of a desire for these things, are we even halfway prepared to pay the penalty? Or when brought before the tribunal do we simply say, "Leave me alone. I am not really guilty. What could I do? I am no worse than anyone else, and better than many. What I do, why, everyone does it. And the things I do not do, well, who's to tell me that anything I might do could ever make a difference anyway? Besides, I've got my own worries to think about. Forget about me. Keep Barabbas."

And ninety-nine out of a hundred times the judge will say, "Fine." The judge will keep Barabbas or opt for any one of a thousand other outs or excuses. The judge will do this for us, because we are the judge.

Every time we plead innocent on advice by the devil's counsel, we are convicted by the gospel—not the devil's good news, but the good news of Jesus. *Love your enemy. Forgive those who persecute you. Empty yourself. Chance your life. Put your trust in the hands of God. Dare to suffer. And dare to fail. Suffer well and fail boldly in causes that are just. And when you've failed in causes that are not, then accept forgiveness and set forth anew.* Such failure, despite all the pain that facing up to it entails, is far more redemptive than much, even most of that which the world celebrates as success.

One final thing.

Jesus preached his gospel with the full expectation that the world was about to end. He called upon his followers to repent and love even their enemies, not to save the world but to ensure that they themselves would have a place in the kingdom.

Today, the same radical ethic demands something more: that we repent and love our enemies—not only to save ourselves, but also to save them.

7. A Natural Diabology

Hell is other people.
                    JEAN PAUL SARTRE

Hell is oneself.
                    T. S. ELIOT

My son Twig and I went to the Bronx Zoo in February, on Lincoln's birthday. We traveled uptown on the subway and got off at the wrong station, turning a merely adventuresome day into a small adventure. The paths were hidden and we did not know the way, but with a little luck and some fairly accurate directions, we trekked from the station across snow-covered fields and entered the zoo from the Bronxdale gate. This put us in the vicinity of the bird house. If zoos are by definition unnatural places, the bird house is perhaps the most unnatural place in a zoo. In any event, we paid the birds a brief visit. Upon reentering the outdoors we spotted a bison—which was encouraging—then found our way to the main gate, and walked up the steps into the central plaza. We wandered for almost half an hour before we encountered another human being.

Zoos without people are unutterably strange places. As far as I could tell, most of the animals didn't mind. Only the monkeys. When we arrived in the monkey house, all was still. But as we began to walk by the cages the monkeys came to life. Hallelujah, finally an audience.

They jumped through tires. They swung on ropes. They hung upside down by their feet on the front of their cages.

Quickly bored, Twig and I went on to the cafeteria. It turned out that all the people visiting the zoo were in the cafeteria having lunch. It was like a cage full of human beings.

"What is your favorite animal so far?" I asked Twig. He pointed out the window at a black squirrel sitting on the roof next door. For a while she watched us with interest, then leaped into a tree and disappeared. I had to admit, in a way that squirrel was more interesting even than the monkeys. Perhaps it is because she was free. "I wish it were summer," Twig said.

This strange mix—birds, monkeys, the squirrel, freedom, summer, my six-year-old son—reminded me of something. Remember how as a child you would long for the coming of summer? By February, the very thought of summer was so sweet you could almost taste it. For me, summer meant freedom: freedom from school; freedom from indoors; even freedom from my parents for a few choice weeks. How I would pray for summer to come.

And when it finally did come, do you remember what happened then? I can recall many good things about summer, but I also remember the disappointment. So clearly I remember sitting with Jimmy Bruce, my best friend, on the stoop of my house in Boise almost any midsummer day.

"Do you want to play baseball?"

"Na, I'm tired of playing baseball."

"So am I." Long pause. "We could play soldiers, but we did that yesterday."

"How about Monopoly?"

"It takes too long."

And so we sat, plumped up in the very lap of summer, bored to tears, nothing to do, no responsibilities, free as birds but nowhere to fly, two little boys sighing on the stoop, budding existentialists weighed down by the burden of time on our hands and the freedom to do with it what we would. We could have done anything we wanted, but couldn't find anything we wanted to do.

And then we grew up. We grew up tempted to do only what we wanted to do, to give just what we felt like giving, to go only where we cared to go.

We called it freedom.

As C. S. Lewis says of the devil: "Satan's monomaniac concern with himself and his supposed rights and wrongs is a necessity of the Satanic predicament. Certainly, he has no choice. He has chosen to have no choice. He has wished to 'be himself,' and to be in himself and for himself, and his wish had been granted. The Hell he carries with him is, in one sense, a Hell of infinite boredom." Like the devil, we are not squirrels running wild, we are not monkeys in a cage, we are little girls and boys sitting on the stoop.

On the other hand, freedom—the freedom to choose— is also the one necessary precondition for virtue. To paraphrase Montaigne, without temptation there is no virtue. For instance, if you are not tempted by alcohol, there is no virtue in the fact that you are not a drunkard. In this sense good and evil slip in and out of one another's costumes, with freedom as the dresser.

"Evil—the Evil One himself—" says one of Thomas Mann's theologians in *Doctor Faustus,* "was a necessary emanation and inevitable accompaniment of the Holy Existence of God, so that vice did not consist in itself but got its satisfaction from the defilement of virtue, without which it would have been rootless; in other words, it consisted in the enjoyment of freedom, the possibility of sinning, which was inherent in the act of creation itself."

Think for a moment about the creation.

The important thing to remember is not that Adam and Eve are created "good" and then fall and become "evil." Rather, it is that they are created "free." The sequence is creation, instruction, temptation, sin, and fall. According to this myth, the fall did not bring evil into the world. Evil was present in potential form within the creation itself. The tree of the knowledge of good and evil is in the garden from the beginning. It is God's tree. When Adam and Eve are tempted by the devil and eat of the fruit of this tree, the dual potential for good and evil in their own nature— in the creation itself—is made manifest to them. They gain the knowledge of it. It is when they fall that they gain direct knowledge of evil, and also of good.

So when the *Book of Common Prayer* says that "There is no health in us," it is wrong, for God is in us. And when liberal theologians blame the corruptions of human nature wholly on environment and not on heredity, they too are wrong, for the devil is in us as well. As Jeffrey Burton Russell writes in his book *The Devil:*

The old liberal belief that man is somehow, for some reason, intrinsically good, and that evils can be corrected by adjusting education, penal laws, welfare arrangements, city planning, and so on, has not proved its validity. Recognition of the basic existence of evil, and consequently of the need for strong efforts to integrate and overcome it, may be socially more useful as well as intellectually and psychologically more true. Further, theists at least should again consider a natural diabology. If a natural theology can be argued from the putative universal human experience of the good, then a natural diabology can be argued from the putative universal human experience of evil.

Indeed.

During my first year in the ministry, I hosted a gathering

for the president of a liberal seminary. Here is what he had
to say about the crisis of our times. There are two kinds of
people, healers and killers. Four percent of all people are
healers. Should we reach the magic threshold of 6 percent,
the world would be saved. Or so he said.

In a way he is right. There is abundant evidence of
healers and killers in our midst. But there is only one kind
of person. We are each healer and killer, sheep and goat.

As Edward Fitzgerald writes:

> I sent my Soul through the Invisible,
> Some letter of that After-life to spell.
> And by and by my Soul return'd to me,
> And answered, "I Myself am Heaven and Hell."

Sooner or later, it all comes home.

In Dostoevski's *The Brothers Karamazov,* there are three
brothers. We have met Ivan, the rationalist, skeptic, atheist,
and social utopian. The other two brothers are something
less (or more) than fully human. They are archetypes.
Alyosha personifies the ideal of active love. Dmitry has
singularly inherited his father's sensuality. Neither is as
familiar or interesting as Ivan, who is by far the most
inwardly divided. It is he, of course, who wrestles with the
devil.

Awakening his brother, the innocent Alyosha, to the terrible reality of evil, he offers these two graphic examples:

Imagine a trembling mother with her baby in her arms, a circle
of invading Turks around her. They've planned a diversion. They
pet the baby, laugh to make it laugh. They succeed, the baby
laughs. At that moment a Turk points a pistol four inches from
the baby's face. The baby laughs with glee, holds out its little
hands to the pistol, and he pulls the trigger in the baby's face

and blows out its brains. Artistic, wasn't it? . . . I think that if the Devil doesn't exist, but man has created him, he has created him in his own image and likeness.

And this.

There was a little girl of five [who] was subjected to every possible torture by [her] cultivated parents. [They] shut her up all night in the cold and frost in a privy, and because she didn't ask to be taken up at night [and so wet herself], they smeared her face and filled her mouth with excrement, and it was her mother, her mother did this. And that mother could sleep, hearing the poor child's groans! Can you understand why a little creature, who can't even understand what's done to her, should beat her little aching heart with her tiny fist in the dark and the cold, and weep her meek unresentful tears to dear, kind God to protect her? . . . Why should mankind know that diabolical good and evil when it costs so much? Why, the whole world of knowledge is not worth that child's prayer to "dear, kind God!"

Ivan shakes his fist at God. Before his very eyes he sees the devil, God, and the tree of the knowledge of good and evil. Unable to deal with any of this rationally, he dismisses all three. They make no sense, so they must not exist.

The fact of blatant and grotesque evil is often used to argue against God's existence. And the argument is completely effective, so long as God by definition is wholly good—dear and kind. But, despite the Teutonic interplay of *Gott* and *gut,* God is not wholly good. The many theoretical explanations for evil in the world that leave God out are neither empirically nor scripturally sound. Evil is not only in us, it is in God and the creation as well. We must begin, however, not with God but with ourselves. If the ancient models for imagining God's nature fail us, we are simply called upon anew to divine from our own experi- ence and according to contemporary metaphors what God's nature might be.

One possibility is suggested by the holograph. The hol- ograph works in conjunction with a laser, which initially beams a split ray of light, half directly to a photo plate and half reflected off an object and then to the photo plate. The photo plate itself consists of thousands of small overlapping circles. After the holograph is taken, a hologram is then reproduced by again directing a laser beam through the plate. The resulting image is a three-dimensional figure that seems to hover in mid-air.

Few practical applications have been found for this ex- traordinary new technology; but as a model for projecting what God might be, the holograph proves, metaphorically at least, quite functional. The reason is this. Mysteriously, if the photographic plate is broken to bits, each bit, if dimly, will still reproduce the whole image. Thus the whole is to found in all the parts.

The holograph offers an image of God that expresses itself neither through subjective experience (pietism) nor through a kind of cool objectivity (rationalism), but, rather, reflexively. The hologram offers one possible clue to deci- phering the nature of reality. Even as our bodies are holo- graphic, with each single cell containing the genetic code for our entire organism, perhaps the universe too is con- tained holographically in our minds.

Despite the modern technological metaphor, there is nothing particularly new about this idea. Pantheism and panentheism, which hold that God is everything or is in everything, can each be interpreted according to this same analogue. Moreover, process theology—in which God is viewed in a wholly natural way as a co-creator with us, as together we move freely toward an undetermined destiny— is also suggestive of the holographic model. Beyond this the hologram offers room for both a personal and imper- sonal dimension to God's being; it allows for God's being both immanent and transcendent, both within us and be- yond us; and it suggests the way in which God's nature, containing both good and evil, might naturally be repli- cated in our own.

By this model, created in the image of God we contain God in the same way that a single cell contains the signa- ture of our whole being. But remember, the devil is also part of God, God's shadow side. If we contain the code for God, the devil too is coded in the helix of our mind. Having tasted the fruit of the tree of the knowledge of good and evil, we gain not only knowledge, but self-knowledge. To know oneself even slightly is to know the devil. To know oneself well is to know both the devil and God.

This is not a dualistic world view, one in which two equal and independent powers—Good and Evil, God and the Devil—struggle for supremacy in the battle for posses- sion of our souls. There is only one God, not two. The devil is a lower-case power, not the picture itself, but dots on the screen that contribute to its composition.

The worst thing about dualism is that it denigrates the earth (which we know) by elevating heaven (which we don't). Sin and flesh become one and the same; body and spirit, opposites—the former the devil's province, the latter that of God. The world-hating, life-denying theologies of fundamentalists everywhere—Shiite Muslims, right-wing Jews, born-again Christians—are dangerous precisely to the extent that they promote a simplified, dualistic vision of reality, God on one side of the fence, the devil on the other. What they fail to recognize is that God's tent is pitched in the enemy's backyard, even as the devil's is in their own.

Every theology that elevates one people or tribe over another, that depends upon purity from every taint of worldly contamination, that posits the condemnation of others as a pledge in earnest for one's own election, is a demonic theology. The earth may be the Lord's, but most religion on this planet today—and from time immemorial—belongs to the devil.

Irreligion fares no better.

Consider the smug, tolerant, rational, wry, independent-minded atheist. His life is a little like a dinner conversation about the weather or the food or the events of the day, anything to help him fill the emptiness and make it through the meal. He may be a good talker, but it doesn't really matter, because nothing really matters more than anything else.

Admittedly, the skeptic may not be quite as tempted as the true believer to persecute his companions—a word that means "those with whom we break bread"—for disagreeing with him; but as far as the devil's concerned that's about all that can be said against him.

Saint Paul had his number: he is spittle, good for nothing but moistening his own tongue. He saves room for dessert, but dessert never comes.

Returning one last time to *The Brothers Karamazov,* the most telling point of Ivan's discourse on evil, the devil, and God turns out to be something very different than why evil exists. When the devil finally appears to Ivan in his dreams, he's not a marauding Turk or a child abuser, but an almost completely innocuous character: petty, eminently forgettable, opinionated, and self-absorbed. When Ivan meets the devil he meets an atheist, a gentleman, a utopian—in fact he meets his own dark side.

The atheist's problem is not all that different from that of the true believer. Each indulges in the devil's favorite sin, the sin of pride. Each worships a little god: in one case a petty, mean-spirited tribal baron; in the other a god even more paltry if no less demonic, the grubby little ego, the god of self. By elevating themselves to a position of philosophical or theological superiority, by claiming knowledge that cannot be had, both atheist and true believer—fundamentalists of the left and right—are estranged, almost by definition, from any true sense of the intimate, awesome, mysterious connectedness, beyond knowing or naming, of all who are born, live, and then die.

Fundamentalists of the left and right may have one another to damn, but when the devil takes the hindmost, he will have a claw for each. And for you and me as well. In his rallying cry for the American revolution, Benjamin Franklin said, "If we don't hang together, we will all hang separately." Today, if we continue to hang separately, each of us clinging to our own narrow creed or anti-creed, it will not be long before we all hang together on the gallows of Armageddon.

The final war will not be a war between the children of light and the children of darkness. It will be what it always has been: a war within the children of life between the powers of light and darkness that dwell within each of us. Until the powers of light begin to prevail in our own lives, the world will not be safe from us and we shall not be safe from one another or ourselves.

From a God's-eye view, it may not matter all that much. Remember how tiny we are, and how limited our understanding. Go out some night and look at the stars. Before them, we are nothing but ants on the cosmic picnic ground.

But for us and for our fellow creatures, our lives matter. We are the ones who have been placed here as stewards, to tend the earth and keep it. We are the ones who have eaten from God's tree, the tree of the knowledge of good and evil—a mixed privilege, but our own. God may be paying precious little attention, but for us and our experiment of life upon this planet, how we act upon our freedom, for good and ill, could not matter more.

There is always hope. So long as we survive there will continue to be hope. If we acknowledge our own complicity in sin; confess the evil in ourselves and celebrate the good in others; show reverence for life, for the interconnected web of all being; banish pride with humility; and act with greatest urgency against the only enemy we have any real power over—the enemy within us—this hope may even grow.

I take particular solace from the story of Peter, perhaps the most paradoxical in all the Bible. After numerous failures both of character and understanding, Peter is dismissed by Jesus with these searing words: "Get thee behind me, Satan" (Matt. 16:23). And yet, in the same chapter Jesus says to him: "Thou art Peter, and upon this rock I shall found my church" (16:18 KJV).

We are Peter.

Epilogue

I am alone in a brightly lighted room. It is furnished with hopes and broken dreams, with honors and failures, open and hidden, from yesterday and long ago. It is my life, and everywhere I look I see some token of myself. Crooked pictures on the wall. Trophies. Unfulfilled expectations. Unexpected fulfillment. And, of course, there are stacks of books, the books of my life, which remain unopened or only half-read, tales of who I might be packaged in the tattered covers of who I am. Behind me, high up on the shelves, there are those unwanted memories, deeds done in haste or left undone. On the desk there are lists, vows to change, new year's resolutions, lists on top of lists, most hidden from view but not forgotten, the folded corners and yellowed edges of my past. And, finally, on the table, right before my eyes but just out of reach, is tomorrow's paper, or next year's, or some year after that, open to the obituary page.

I am sitting in a chair in the middle of this brightly lit room that is my life, and what am I doing? I am looking out of a window. It is my window on good and evil, on meaning, on truth, on the mystery of life and death. It is my window on God. Once again I am trying to make sense of what it means to be alive and then to die.

There is only one problem. It is very bright in my room, and very dark outside. And so all I see in this window is a reflection of myself and my life. I see the crooked pictures, the unwashed dishes, the unread books. I see my own familiar, yet forbidding reflection in the glass. My window upon meaning is a mirror. My life is back-lit, and when I look out my window seeking truth or meaning or God, all I see is my own reflection and the litter of my life in the glass.

But then I turn out the lights. It is a little frightening at first. However bad things are it is always reassuring to see our own reflection, to know that we are there. When we turn out the lights in the apartment of our lives, we cannot see ourselves in the window. It is no longer a mirror. We sit in complete darkness.

But look closely. On the other side of the window things begin to happen. The stars come out. I don't know what they mean, but there they are, right there shining through our window, awesome, mysterious, dancing in our eyes. We become very small in contrast to the wonder—the miracle of life and death, love and loss, joy and pain—in contrast to the overarching mystery.

This sense of smallness is perhaps our best protection against the devil. Not that it makes us feel pointless or ineffectual. It doesn't. It just helps us take ourselves more lightly and the cosmos more seriously. When we turn off the lights and look through the window a connection is made. The moment is invested with eternity.

Or can be.

Every house of worship has its windows also. What do we see when we look through them? Do we see God? Or is it pictures of God we see, drawn to satisfy our own prejudices?

And what do we hear? Do we hear the soundings of the universe, mysterious, awesome, humbling? Or is it words we have put in God's mouth, the devil's gospel, assuring us that our salvation cries for others to be damned?

Long ago, St. Ignatius wrote a book on *Rules for the Discernment of Spirits*. For example, a woman is speaking in tongues. Is it God speaking through her, or is it the devil? Most of the time, of course, the tongues we speak in are our own. Even so, when we speak or act, even with great confidence in the clarity of our words or rightness of our deeds, there is still a need for discernment of spirits. Since both God and the devil have a way of turning up where we least expect to find them, to distinguish good from evil in our own daily lives is often more difficult than at first it might appear.

The main problem is that we more readily distinguish evil in other people, institutions, governments, social and economic orders, than we can in our own lives or religion or politics. And when we do recognize it in own lives— each of us having that part of ourself that we especially regret and despise—it tends to be the obvious flaws, sins of the flesh or weaknesses of the spirit, for which we hate ourselves.

But the devil's specialty is not lust, sloth, or gluttony. Nor is it paralyzing shyness, insecurity, social awkwardness, or any of those things for which God would dearly love us if only we would allow it. No, the devil's specialty is evil disguised as good.

Take this book, for instance. I wrote it during the month of July while in California on a family vacation. I can assure you that, although it is not a long book, it filled the days of July—morning, afternoon, and night—handsomely.

For me, that is. I also have a wife and two children.

Everything we do, however highly esteemed by others,

has evil consequences. There are no exceptions. This is why paradox is potentially such a useful tool.

Though far from being a final solution to short-sightedness or self-absorption, paradox will almost always expand our vistas. And so I invite you, as you leave this little book on the devil, to ponder not your most obvious sins, but the attitudes, opinions, and actions you exult in. Remember, Satan fell from heaven on account of pride.

Try this idolatry test.

1. *Do you pride yourself on your social conscience, concern for others, love for humanity?*
   Have you called your mother lately?

2. *Do you pride yourself on your knowledge of current events, read all the right magazines, watch the news twice a day?*
   Did you vote in the last municipal election? Did you write to your congressperson about his or her stand on arms control? Perhaps you ought to boycott the paper for a day or two and read a trashy novel, one you couldn't mention in proper company. It might do you good.

3. *Do you pride yourself on your honesty, high sense of purpose, and dependability? Do you come to work early and stay late?*
   Call in sick at once. Go directly to a ball game or a B-movie. The work will go on without you. The question is, can you go on without the work?

4. *Do you pride yourself in your health, take good care of your body, eat well, exercise, drink to moderation, never smoke?*

   Fine. There may be any number of good reasons to do this, but living forever doesn't qualify.

5. *Do you pride yourself on your patriotism?*

   Please—for my sake as well as your own—find a blacklist somewhere and get on it. The odds are this will serve the country you love far better.

6. *Do you take pride in your religiosity? Do you go to church or synagogue every weekend?*

   If so, skip a week or, better, skip a month. And while you're gone, ask yourself: "Should I go back?"

Idolatry tests are useful, because pride is far more blind than love.

I suppose that's all I really have to say. Watch out for the people in white, they may be Klansmen. And beware of sirens, however sweet their song. For the devil takes what is attractive and makes it fatally so. To squeeze the devil out, sometimes all that is required is a little less of a good thing.

Remember, the Church of the Beatitudes in Nazareth was funded by Mussolini.

And remember Huck Finn, when he decides not to collect a bounty by turning Jim in as a runaway slave: "I was a-trembling because I'd got to decide forever betwixt two things, and I knowed it. I studied for a minute, sort of holding my breath, and then says to myself, 'All right, then, I'll go to Hell.'"

Sources

AUTHOR'S PREFACE

p. ix **"I wanted to"** Jakob Boehme, cited by Maximillian Rudwin, *The Devil in Legend and Literature* (Chicago: Open Court, 1931), 8.

p. x **"The prince of"** William Shakespeare, *King Lear* III, iv, 148.

p. x **"Angels can fly"** G. K. Chesterton, *Orthodoxy* (Garden City, N.Y.: Image, 1959), 120.

1. THE CARE AND FEEDING OF THE DEVIL

p. 1 **"Evil is terribly"** Carl Jung, "Good and Evil in Analytical Psychology," in *The Collected Works of Carl G. Jung*, translated by R. F. C. Hull, Bollingen Series XX (Princeton: Princeton University Press, 1964), 465.

p. 3 **"There is no"** Walt Kelly, *We Have Met the Enemy and He Is Us* (New York: Fireside, 1972).

p. 5 **"Though with their"** William Shakespeare, *The Tempest* V, i, 25–27.

p. 5 **"is the great"** E. M. W. Tillyard, *The Elizabethan World Picture* (New York: Vintage, n.d.), 72

2. WELCOME TO HELL

p. 8 **"The safest road"** C. S. Lewis, *The Screwtape Letters* (New York: Macmillan, 1948), 65.

p. 10–11 **"By throwing into . . . into the background."** Nathaniel Hawthorne, "The Celestial Rail-road," in *Tales and Sketches* (New York: Library of America, 1982), 809–810.

p. 12 **"I look around"** Nathaniel Hawthorne, "The Minister's Black Veil," Ibid., 384.

p. 12 **"The scientific superiority"** Thomas Mann, *Doctor Faustus,* translated by H. T. Lowe-Porter (New York: Alfred A. Knopf, 1963), 90.

p. 13 **"It is characteristic"** Henry Fairlie, *The Seven Deadly Sins Today* (Washington: New Republic, 1978), 15–16.

p. 14 **"relegated to the"** W. E. Gladstone, *Studies Subsidiary to the Works of Bishop Butler*, 1898, 206, cited by Geoffrey Rowell, *Hell and the Victorians* (Oxford: Clarendon, 1974), 212.

p. 15 **"in New York"** Ambrose Bierce, *The Devil's Dictionary* (New York: Albert and Charles Boni, 1925), 162.

p. 16 **"the night less"** Meg Greenfield, "Heart of Darkness," *Newsweek* (Dec. 4, 1978): 132.

p. 17 **"The argument that"** B. F. Skinner, interviewed by Elizabeth Mehren, "A Utopian Succumbs to Pessimism," *Philadelphia Inquirer* (Sept. 25, 1982): C3.

3. THE CUNNING LIVERY OF HELL

p. 18 **"Had he been"** Daniel Defoe, *The History of the Devil* (Totowa, N.J.: Rowman and Littlefield, [1819] 1972), 244.

p. 18 **"The Devil's most"** Charles Baudelaire, *Petits Poèmes en Prose* XXIX, 75.

p. 19 **"He is at"** Jakob Grimm, cited by Maximillian Rudwin, *Devil in Legend and Literature* (Chicago: Open Court, 1931), 3.

p. 20 **"Discoverie of Witchcraft"** Reginald Scot, *The Discoverie of Witchcraft* (London: J. Rodker, [1584] 1930).

p. 20 **"Black appears as"** Arturo Graf, *The Story of the Devil*, translated by Edward Noble Stone (New York: Macmillan, 1931), 28.

p. 22 **"I thought to"** Federigo Frezzi, *Quadriregio,* cited Ibid., 32.

p. 26 **"Majestic though in"** John Milton, *Paradise Lost* II, 305; II, 44–45.

p. 27 **"With Grave Aspect"** John Milton, *Paradise Lost* II, 305; II, 44–45; II, 300–304.

p. 27 **"The perfect impersonation"** Marie Corelli, *The Sorrows of Satan* (New York: American News, 1903), 470.

p. 27 **"He made us"** Mark Twain, "The Mysterious Stranger," in *The Portable Mark Twain,* edited by Bernard De Voto (New York: Viking, 1983), 643.

p. 28 **"Either the Devil"** Defoe, *History of the Devil*, 279–280.

p. 28 **"There is a"** Hal Lindsey, *Satan Is Alive and Well on Planet Earth* (New York: Bantam, 1974), 14.

p. 28 **"Satan does not"** Billy Graham, *Approaching Hoofbeats: The Four Horsemen of the Apocalypse* (Waco, Texas: Word Books, 1983), 104.

4. IDOLATRIES OF GOOD

p. 30 **"And out of"** Milton, *Paradise Lost* I, 165.

p. 30 **"honor, dominion, glory,"** Milton, *Paradise Lost* VI, 422.

p. 31 **"In the world"** Dorothy Sayers, "The Other Six Deadly Sins," in *Creed or Chaos?* (New York: Harcourt, Brace, 1949), 81.

p. 31 **"Love seeketh not . . . in Heaven's despite."** William Blake, "The Clod and the Pebble," 1–4, 9–12.

p. 32 **"Culture which the"** Johann Wolfgang von Goethe, *Faust*, First Part (London: J. Wacey, 1839), scene VI, 281.

p. 33 **"Not conforming to"** Ambrose Bierce, *The Devil's Dictionary* (New York: Albert and Charles Boni, 1925), 12.

p. 35 **"In this world"** Oscar Wilde, *Lady Windermere's Fan*, in *Comedies by Oscar Wilde* (New York: Book League of America, 1932), Act III, 127.

p. 38 **"Men never do"** Blaise Pascal, *Pensées*, 813.

p. 38 **"The devil can"** William Shakespeare, *The Merchant of Venice* I, iii, 99.

p. 38 **"Handel's music and"** George Bernard Shaw, *The Devil's Disciple,* in *Selected Plays* (New York: Dodd, Mead, 1898), Act III, 340.

p. 39 **"The need to"** Desmond Tutu, cited by Michael Parks, "Tutu Stops Mob from Burning Man to Death," *Los Angeles Times* (July 11, 1985): Pt. I, 12.

p. 39 **"whose Liberal-Protestant"** Aldous Huxley, *Ape and Essence* (New York: Harper & Brothers, 1948), 194, 126.

p. 39 **"dark with excessive"** Milton, *Paradise Lost* III, 380.

p. 40 **"With devotion's visage"** William Shakespeare, *Hamlet* III, i, 47.

5. THE DEVIL AND THE FUTURE

p. 42 **"Linehart [entering]: Victory"** Jean Paul Sartre, *The Devil & The Good Lord* (New York: Alfred A. Knopf, 1960), Act I, 4.

p. 43 **"famous book in"** Ambrose Bierce, *The Devil's Dictionary* (New York: Albert and Charles Boni, 1925), 292.

p. 44 **"Russia is a"** Hal Lindsey, *The Late Great Planet Earth* (New York: Bantam, 1973).

p. 45 **"wanted to come . . . good and evil"** Fyodor Dostoevski, *The Brothers Karamazov*, translated by Andrew H. MacAndrew (New York: Bantam, 1970), 298–313.

p. 48 **"I tell you . . . the earthly paradise"** Aldous Huxley, *Ape and Essence* (New York: Harper & Brothers, 1948), 125–126.

p. 49 **"The United States"** Frank Church, "Introduction" to *Senate Committee on Intelligence Report on Alleged Assassination Plots Against Foreign Leaders*, 1976.

p. 49 **"They acted on"** Frank Church, "Declaration of Candidacy for President," Idaho City, Idaho, March 13, 1976.

p. 50 **"The blood of"** Tertullian, *Apollogy* 50.

p. 50 **"how fragile a"** Sidney Hook, cited by Michael Kinsley, "New Patriots Heap Abuse on America," *The Los Angeles Times* (July 16, 1985): Pt. II, 5.

p. 51 **"not basically structured"** Jean-François Revel, *How Democracies Perish*, translated by William Byron, (Garden City, N.Y.: Doubleday, 1983), 3–4.

p. 51 **"Nations like America"** Michael Kinsley, "New Patriots Heap Abuse on America," *The Los Angeles Times* (July 16, 1985): Pt. II, 5.

p. 52 **"Man's best force"** Friedrich Nietzsche, cited by Maximillian Rudwin, *Devil in Legend and Literature* (Chicago: Open Court, 1931), 279.

p. 52 **"Progress, my lords!"** Upton Sinclair, *Hell* (Pasadena, Calif.: Published by the author, 1923), 43.

p. 52 **"Once every member"** Dostoevsky, *Brothers Karamazov*, 781.

p. 53 **"constantly tempted to"** Reinhold Niebuhr, *Beyond Tragedy* (New York: Charles Scribner's Sons, 1937), 28.

p. 53 **"Even without the"** Huxley, *Ape and Essence*, 123–125.

p. 53 **"Man must and . . . The Natural heart"** William Blake, "Jerusalem," plate 52.

p. 54 **"The Grand Inquisitor"** Dostoevsky, *Brothers Karamazov*, 316.

p. 54 **"If we feel"** Huxley, *Ape and Essence*, 194–195.

6. JESUS AND THE FUTURE

p. 56 **"Gallup poll on"** Kenneth A. Briggs, "Gallup Poll Finds the Image of Jesus to Be Somewhat Murkey," *The New York Times* (Apr. 3, 1983): Pt. I, 15.

p. 59 **"The Quest of"** Albert Schweitzer, *The Quest of the Historical Jesus* translated by W. Montgomery (London: A. & C. Black, 1910).

p. 60 **"The good conscience"** Albert Schweitzer, *Philosophy of Civilization*, translated by C. T. Campion (London: A. & C. Black, 1923), 318.

p. 62 **"In Jesus Christ"** Albert Schweitzer, cited by Richard H. Hiers, *Jesus and Ethics* (Philadelphia: Westminster Press, 1968), 58, 62.

p. 64 **"The future is,"** C. S. Lewis, *The Screwtape Letters* (New York: Macmillan, 1948), 77.

p. 65 **"For all The . . . Behold our enginery!"** Upton Sinclair, *Hell* (Pasadena, Calif: Published by the author, 1923), 40, 42.

p. 65 **"Sins against the"** William F. May, cited by Henry Fairlie, *The Seven Deadly Sins Today* (Washington: New Republic, 1978), 144.

7. A NATURAL DIABOLOGY

p. 73 **"Hell is other"** Jean Paul Sartre, *No Exit*, in *No Exit and The Flies*, translated by Stuart Gilbert (New York: Alfred A. Knopf, 1954), 61.

p. 73 **"Hell is oneself"** T. S. Eliot, *The Cocktail Party* (New York: Harcourt, Brace, 1950), 98.

p. 75 **"Satan's monomaniac concern"** C. S. Lewis, *A Preface to Paradise Lost* (New York: Oxford University Press, 1961), 102.

p. 75 **"Evil—the Evil"** Thomas Mann, *Dr. Faustus*, translated by H. T. Lowe-Porter (New York: Alfred A. Knopf, 1963), 100.

p. 76 **"There is no"** *The Book of Common Prayer*, "Morning Prayer, A General Confession," 6.

p. 76 **"The old liberal"** Jeffrey Burton Russell, *The Devil: Perceptions of Evil from Antiquity to Primitive Christianity* (Ithaca, N.Y.: Cornell, 1977), 260.

p. 77 **"I sent my"** Edward Fitzgerald, *The Rubaiyat of Omar Khayyam* LXVI.

p. 77 **"Imagine a trembling . . . dear, kind God!"** Dostoevski, *The Brothers Karamazov*, Book V, Chapter 4, cited by Russell in *The Devil*.

EPILOGUE

p. 88 **"I was a-trembling"** Mark Twain, *Huckleberry Finn*, in *The Portable Mark Twain*, edited by Bernard de Voto (New York: Viking, 1983), 451.